ADVANCE PRAISE FOR

Technology, Culture, and Socioeconomics

"With this book, Patricia A. O'Riley engages an interdisciplinary audience with an important and highly original analysis of the cultural significance of the ubiquitously utopian, Eurocentric, technocratic discourses that abound in the current race to 'get connected and share in the dream.' O'Riley's polyvocal text weaves together aboriginal, postcolonial, and postmodern languages, locations, and worldviews that, in its performativity, is as powerfully dramaturgical as it is expository. *Technology, Culture, and Socioeconomics* should be required reading for every educator in need of a new lens for thinking critically about digital technologies, for researchers struggling to find a way through the paralyzing maze of postmodern deconstruction, and for all of us marginals who, against all odds, toil away in the e-sweatshops of education in the twenty-first century thinking and feeling that we might actually figure out how to hack a virus capable of derailing the neoliberal newspeak that threatens to silence and extinguish all signs of intelligent life in the universe. O'Riley's brilliant text gives us some really good code to get that virus into circulation."

—*Mary Bryson, Professor of Education,*
University of British Columbia, Canada

"If, as Umberto Eco writes, a novel is a machine for generating interpretations, then *Technology, Culture, and Socioeconomics* is a plant (ambiguous homonym intentional!) that regenerates interpretations of technology education. But Patricia A. O'Riley also reimagines and reinvents the plant/machine itself. Like a post-structuralist textual equivalent of Charles Babbage's 'difference engine,' O'Riley's rhizoanalytic method runs in perpetual e-motion, continually deconstructing, decolonizing, reforming, and transforming the technocultural discourses-practices that she tracks and traces. With frequent interruptions from Coyote (and an unruly cast of fellow tricksters and travelers), O'Riley's new tales of technology education are intellectually rigorous and serious without being solemn; some are perplexing and unsettling; some will make you laugh out loud; all are utterly compelling."

—*Noel Gough, Professor of Education,*
Deakin University, Australia

Technology, Culture, and Socioeconomics

Studies in the Postmodern Theory of Education

Joe L. Kincheloe and Shirley R. Steinberg
General Editors

Vol. 216

PETER LANG
New York • Washington, D.C./Baltimore • Bern
Frankfurt am Main • Berlin • Brussels • Vienna • Oxford

PATRICIA A. O'RILEY

Technology, Culture, and Socioeconomics

A Rhizoanalysis of Educational Discourses

PETER LANG
New York • Washington, D.C./Baltimore • Bern
Frankfurt am Main • Berlin • Brussels • Vienna • Oxford

Library of Congress Cataloging-in-Publication Data

O'Riley, Patricia A. (Patricia Ann).
Technology, culture, and socioeconomics: a rhizoanalysis
of educational discourses / Patricia A. O'Riley.
p. cm. — (Counterpoints; v. 216)
Includes bibliographical references and index.
1. Educational technology. 2. Critical pedagogy. 3. Discourse analysis, Narrative.
4. Multicultural education. 5. Postmodernism and education. I. Title: Technology,
culture, and socioeconomics. II. Title. III. Counterpoints (New York, N.Y.); v. 216.
LB1028.3 .O73   371.33—dc21   2002034909
ISBN 0-8204-5793-0
ISSN 1058-1634

Bibliographic information published by **Die Deutsche Bibliothek**.
Die Deutsche Bibliothek lists this publication in the "Deutsche
Nationalbibliografie"; detailed bibliographic data is available
on the Internet at http://dnb.ddb.de/.

Cover design by Joni Holst

The paper in this book meets the guidelines for permanence and durability
of the Committee on Production Guidelines for Book Longevity
of the Council of Library Resources.

© 2003 Peter Lang Publishing, Inc., New York
275 Seventh Avenue, 28th Floor, New York, NY 10001
www.peterlangusa.com

All rights reserved.
Reprint or reproduction, even partially, in all forms such as microfilm,
xerography, microfiche, microcard, and offset strictly prohibited.

Printed in the United States of America

Contents

Acknowledgments	vii
PREAMBLE	1
Unfolding Technology Discourses in Education	4
Technology Discourses as Manifest Manners	7
One Woman's Story	12
Writing Plateaux	17
Topographical Legend	21
RE: MAPPING	23
Rhizomatics	24
Rhizomatics Meet Trickster Discourse	33
Chance Operations, Poethics, and Silence	36
MESA MORPHING METHODOLOGY	41
Framing Methodology	42
Validity as Incitement to Discourse	48
Coming Out of the *Co*-Closet	50
SITING TECH ED	55
The ~~Ford~~ Four Model Ts, or the Technification of Tech Ed	56
Control(ling) Technology	59
Tech Ed as Capital Ad/venture	65
SHAPESHIFTING TECH ED	75
Remembering Tech Ed's Gendered and Industrial Roots	76
Virtual Silence on Environment	83
Te(a)ching Us and Them	86
Interrupting Neocolonialism	89
Knotting Columbus	95

VIRTUAL(LY) ED TECH	99
Cyborgology	101
Cyborgs in Education	104
First World Netscape and Third World Landscape?	106
Tricksteria Pre/re/figures Cyborgia	116
A DATAPLAY	121
Ludic Encounters	**122**
JOINING LANDSCAPE AND EPISTEMOLOGIES	143
Telling Different Stories	144
Equivalency of Epistemologies	150
References	159
Index	173

Acknowledgments

This book would not have been possible without the technology education students and their teacher, the educational technology graduate students, and my friend and colleague, mutindi ndunda, whose words enliven and add much wisdom to its pages. I would also like to thank the theorists whose work provided inspiration, hope, and delight, especially Gilles Deleuze, Félix Guattari, John Cage, Gerald Vizenor, and Donna Haraway. I am grateful to my thesis committee, Patti Lather, Bill Taylor, and Bob Donmoyer, for giving me the space in which I was able to do experimental work. Heidi Burns, Senior Editor, and Bernadette Shade, Production Coordinator, I want to thank you for your valuable assistance in getting the manuscript to this stage. Many thanks for the love and support of my children, their partners, and my grandchildren: Lee and Derek; Chris; Lori, Ted, Amber, and Jessica; and, my sisters, Lorraine and Kym. Dear friends and colleagues also played a supportive role. Thank you to all of you, and a special thanks to Len Millis, Mary Bryson, Annette Gough, Noel Gough, Donna Trueit, Bill Doll, Steve Petrina, and Chris Bastone. I thank my partner, Peter Cole, for his loving support, as well as his wise and witty tricksterisms throughout the book. This writing journey would not have taken the shape that it has without his encouragement to write from my heart. I also thank the Creator for the gifts I have been given, and the space and opportunity for the meetings and experiences that have lead to the researching and writing of this book.

I gratefully thank the editors of the *Journal of Technology Education* and the *Australian Educational Researcher* for their permission to excerpt and paraphrase from articles that I have previously published with them:

> O'Riley, P. (1996). A different storytelling of technology education curriculum re-visions: A storytelling of difference. *Journal of Technology Education*, 7(2), 28–39.

O'Riley, P., & Scott, D. (1996). Psycho logics: Techno bits and desire bytes in the worlds of virtuality and analysis. *Australian Educational Researcher*, 23(3), 97–107.

Preamble

> The problem is not to put up bridges between already fully constituted and fully delimited domains, but to put in place new theoretical and practical machines, capable of sweeping away the old stratifications, and of establishing the conditions for a new exercise in desire.
> —Félix Guattari, *Chaosophy*

The building looks like a factory, a 1960's design constructed to train industrial education teachers. From her locker, which is located in the long dark industrial-green windowless hallway and just outside the male washroom, she pulls her coveralls on over her jeans, laces up her steel-toed boots, picks up her toolbox, and heads to the automotive shop to reassemble a two-stroke combustion engine. There is no locker room for females. There are no other females in the programme. She is partnered with a male student. She can smell the wood in the shop across the hall and wishes that she were there instead. As she enters the automotive shop, two of the students are having trouble getting the brakes off an old Ford they have been restoring for their term project. She notices a girly calendar on the wall. The next class is metal shop. She can hear the high-pitched scream of a metal lathe. Fumes from the welding alcove linger in the air. Some students have already begun working on the toolbox they are to make for the next assignment and are bending sheet metal on a box and pan press.

Today they are to hand in their tool gauges. She had spent a lot of time on hers so that it would have a mirror finish and the edges would be smooth to the touch. The instructor grabs her tool gauge and holds it up as an example of care and attention—to the snickers and disparaging comments of some of her fellow students. She hides her tool gauge in her pocket and looks around for something to stand on so that she can operate the press. It is time to head off to the electronics shop where she solders components for her power supply project. She is not too taken with the pictures the instructor showed yesterday of enclosures, for the power supply units made by the previous years' students. They looked like huge shoeboxes, so she begins sketching some designs that are smaller and aesthetically pleasing, at least to her sensibilities. Lunch cannot come soon enough so that she can get away from the sexist conversation in the next cubicle. It's a constant barrage no matter which shop she is in. It's awful.

After lunch is materials science where the students are testing the density of different wood types. Based on her experiences as an occupational health and safety officer, she speaks to the instructor after class about the unsafe storage of chemicals in the lab. She is invited to talk with the head of the programme, as well as the other instructors, to see if they might be interested in having her do a safety inspection of all the shops. There is considerable resistance from one of the senior instructors. She decides to approach them about the girly calendar in the automotive shop. "You need to get a better grip on things. Remember where you are. If you're going to make it through this programme, you'll need to lighten up!"

She returns to her locker, takes off her coveralls and steel-toed boots, puts on her runners, pulls her AutoCAD disks out of her backpack, and heads to the computer lab. She had just spent almost $5,000 on a 286 computer and computer programmes, including AutoCAD, a huge financial burden for a student, and so she is determined to get the most out of this class, particularly because she has years of experience as a housing designer and is anxious to see if AutoCAD can produce the feeling of aliveness as her own hand drafting can. Her instructor is learning AutoCAD along with the class. She shows him how to insert text.

Tears roll down her cheeks on the drive home. She wonders why the instructors cannot seem to understand that there is nothing between those walls that feels relevant, or warm, or welcoming to females. She wonders at her own naïveté in believing that equity could be more than rhetoric in education. Being a provincial human rights officer was another of the hats that she wore in her former life, and she learned very quickly that the laws are not there to protect those whom they purport to protect. She should know better. She wonders why the instructors, and more importantly the Ministry of Education, cannot see that all the instructors are male and white, and that the curriculum is male and white. It is as if they assume that male and white is the universal default position.

She asks, "How has it come to be that in spite of recent revisions, technology education remains limited to technical and trades-oriented technologies? How has it come to be that a critical and urgent conversation on gender, cultural, socioeconomic, global, and environmental issues in relation to technology is not at the foreground of technology curricula? How has it come to be that technologies associated with everyday living and the home have been pushed to the side? How has it come to be that western technologies are languaged as high, and Indigenous technologies talked about as low, or no, technologies? How is it that there is such an uncritical emphasis on design and making when the earth is suffocating, gasping for breath, amidst the unparalleled production, consumption, and waste of the past fifty years? What other conversations on technology need to become a part of the technology discourses in education today? Who might be able to bring these conversations to the table?"

One of the senior instructors replies angrily, "Where is your common sense? We don't want to throw the baby out with the bath water."

"I agree," she says, "however, the bath water needs to be warmed up a bit, and a much larger bath tub is needed so that there is space for more than a white male baby. Half of the students in schools are females, and more than half of the students in British Columbia schools are of non-European heritage."

He counters, "If my memory serves me well, I believe we have had a couple of Chinese students through the programme. I don't remember any Native students. Anyway, nobody's stopping girls from taking technology education. Besides, a couple of schools have been offering powder-puff mechanics and woodworking for years. Now many of the schools are putting live plants in the new technology labs and repainting the walls with brighter colours to attract girls. We're putting a woman on the Ministry of Education curriculum revision committee. What more do you want?"

Unfolding Technology Discourses in Education

> Any narrative that predetermines all responses or prohibits any counter narratives puts an end to narrative itself by suppressing all possible alternative actions and responses, by making itself its own end and the end of all narratives. (Carroll, 1982, p. 77)

Since the early 1980s there has been a storm of curriculum revisioning in education, with a heavy influence from political /corporate interests. Two principle areas have emerged from the fray to design and disseminate technology discourses: technology education and educational technology. For the most part, the curricula have been designed and implemented without crucial and genuine consultation and dialogue with teachers, students, parents or guardians, and communities. The rhetoric of technology education and educational technology are surprisingly similar—both narratives are momented by a dogma of high tech, production, economic expansion, and inevitability. A major goal of these disciplines is to ensure that students become technologically literate, which translates as little more than 'the learner' becoming an acquiescent producer, consumer, and user of high technologies. Time and space for a critical conversation on technology does not play a central role, if at all.

Depending on the country, province, state, or municipality, revised industrial education curricula have been renamed technology, technology education, technology studies. or technological studies. These revisions have been heralded as constituting a paradigm shift; however, from my positioning I see little more than a re-wiring of industrial education. While the selection of knowledge and technological processes within the revisions are more diverse and more 'high' tech than the previous industrial education curricula, they are still centred on industrial design and making products. Many of the values, assumptions, beliefs, and practices underpinning industrial education, which has historically marginalized or excluded female students and students from a diversity of cultures, remain unproblematized and unchallenged. Rather than remapping space for difference and creating possibilities to realize the rhetoric of 'curricula for all students,' much of the Eurocentric, male, and technicist "persistence of vision" (Haraway, 1989) of the former industrial education curricula has been sustained and retrenched in the revised curricula. Although the revisionings have been done through new high tech frames, sadly the lenses remain unaffected, myopic. Gender, culture, socioeconomics, and the environment are beyond the sightlines, mere optical illusions, rhetorical delusions.

Educational technology (computer technology) is a recent upshoot; the new kid on the block and it has been virtually, and really, gaining momentum and massive amounts of funding over the past two decades. Educational technology, sometimes referred to as information technology, is not always taught as a specific discipline at the primary and secondary education levels, rather as computers across the curriculum. Teachers are encouraged to integrate the use of computer technology into their teaching practices, whereas students are assigned to use computer technology in their learning situations. Enter the partnerships with industry. Political leaders, very much influenced by computer companies and their advocates, are making promises of a laptop for every student. Computers come with extraordinarily huge capital expenditure for classroom (re)construction, hardware, software, teacher training, maintenance, and upgrades that most schools cannot afford. For example, River Oaks School in Oakville, Ontario, once considered to be a model of on-line learning in the early 1990s, now has cupboards and floors filled with obsolete computers (Petricic, 2002). Their annual $500,000 cost for keeping up with computer technology does not match their $70,000 budget. Students are relearning how to read and write using books and their own handwriting. The computers they do have are used as tools, much like pens and pencils, rather than the centre of their learning. Petricic asks the crucial question: Does the technology make a difference? Recent studies are showing that their effectiveness for learning has been highly overestimated. With the growing concerns about obese students like never before, parents are asking that students spend less time on computers and more time doing physical activities. I cannot help but think of the many more urgent and socially responsible uses for these monies.

Brian Massumi (1992), referring to the work of Gilles Deleuze and Félix Guattari, suggests that the content of education plays a largely irrelevant role and is relatively disengaged from how education is expressed. For example, when politicians say that education is to build good citizens, this is not expressed simply through curricular content, but through the making of compliant adolescents to become preprogrammed unquestioning future voters, or taxpayers, at any rate. In the same way, how technology is expressed in education is through complex interrelationships of language, texts and subtexts, practices, environments, and bodies. These "expressibles" take shape as order-words or order(ing) words comprised of statements of commands placing "the concerned body and bodies in a position to carry out implicit obligations or follow a preset direction" (p. 31). Technology discourses are hierarchical and "vertical constructions" whose "terms are defined by reference to already given ideas, established meanings, and corresponding material practices" (Crnkovic, 1994, p. 169). The agenda is set with no room for difference or spontaneity. Students and teachers are to follow prescribed curricula with prescribed learning outcomes and to march without question in the latest imperial progress(ion)—global corporate capitalism. Females, indigenous populations, the poor, and the environment are the silents—the unlistened to, the unheeded—as they become drowned out in the filling in of the conversation by Eurocentric white male noise. Money and power are the carrots—probably genetically modified.

Technology is much more complex, fluid, and ambiguous than design and market production, or learning to use computers and multimedia technologies. Technology plays a significant role in the global revisioning and reshaping of the relationships between and among people, other living things, geographies, epistemologies, and ways of (re)presenting and being in the world. Western technologies are especially implicated in the widening disparity between those who have power to control their own lives and those who do not. Global corporate technocapitalism in its many disguises is increasingly eroding hard-fought gains for human rights, employment equity, labour standards, occupational health and safety, and the environment. Individuals and populations have become resources, commodities, cogs, and part of the machinery and machinations of corporate production. The gap between us and them widens.

My desire is to explore a different technological literacy in education, one that *affirms and celebrates difference*. Considering the manipulations, allegiances, and alliances of global corporate capitalism, as well as its arrangements of capital, technologies, time, space, bodies, and geographies, I question the adequacy of the current technology discourses to represent technology at this historical juncture, especially their relevancy with respect to the gender, cultural, and socioeconomic diversity of students entering today's classrooms, and their responsibility and commitment to the larger society and the environment. My point is *not to deny* the validity of the technology discourses currently offered in schools, but to put forward that they leave out many other realities and technologies that have the potential to enrich the conversation, encourage humility, respect for difference(s), and encourage environmental sensitivity.

Technology Discourses as Manifest Manners

Daniel Quinn in his book, *Ishmael* (1993), allegorizes the human condition through an intellectual journey with Ishmael, a gorilla of immense wisdom, and his acolyte, a white male human. Ishmael says that life in one cage is like life in any other cage and that humans are captives to a civilized system directed inexorably toward destroying the world. The world is captive to human greed, and human beings are unable to find the bars of the cage because the bars are everyday thoughts and daily rituals. They are invisible, subliminal. Western humans, in particular, are captives of an anthropocentric story which is so pervasive, so taken-for-granted, that there is no need to name it or discuss it. Quinn says we (westerners) know the story before entering school, and if we do not, we learn very quickly our place in the story. We see the earth as a human-support system, a machine, a hinterland, a warehouse, a resource depot, designed to sustain, and enhance (some) human life at the expense of (most) other human life and at the expense of other forms of aliveness. Part of the story being taught is that the destiny of humans is to tame and conquer the chaos and wilderness of our world. The world is paying a heavy price for enacting this throughline. Quinn binarises human beings into givers and takers. Givers return something to the earth. Takers only take—and sometimes they *talk about* sustainability, or more often, sustainable development. As though words alone could undo the damage. Quinn argues that western knowledge ends at the border of western culture. If westerners venture beyond that border, they will fall off because their story cannot imagine that there is anything beyond. Comparable to Christopher Columbus and the thousands of discoverers and researchers who followed him, his map, his rules, his vision, his languaging, his religion, his assumptions, takers are not able to imagine, hear, see, or otherwise experience those who live *elsewhere* and *otherwise*. What is invisible on western maps is in plain sight—and seen and lived—for billions of others.

Gerald Vizenor (1994), a Chippewa novelist and professor, writes that imperial imaginings are "manifest manners" having no relations. Similarly, in Thomas King's (1993) delightful story, *A Coyote Columbus Story*, Old Coyote in her/his retelling of the hegemonic story of Christopher Columbus's so-called discovery of America, refers to such imperial imaginings as "bad manners."

> Boy...I must have sung that song wrong. Maybe I didn't do the right dance. Maybe I thought too hard. These people I made have no manners. They act as if they have no relations....But, you know, once you think things like that, you can't take them back. So you have to be careful what you think. (p. 12)

Technologies of First Peoples that have been indispensable cultural enactments for millennia have been *dis*regarded in the imperial Eurocentric "fictive framework of ideological codes, which, like all semiotic systems, are grounded in nothing more than human desire and fear but which appear to have authority of essential truth" (Russell, quoted in Vizenor, 1993, p. 194). Eurocentric cultural framings and universalizing practices perpetuate what John Willinsky (1998) fittingly names as "the legacy of imperialism" in education. They mask what Ella Shohat and Robert Stam (1994) refer to as "linguistics of domination" in Eurocentric historical, sociocultural, and political reconstructions and reproductions.

> The Columbus story is crucial to Eurocentrism, not only because Columbus was a seminal [sic] figure within the history of colonialism, but also

> because idealized versions of his story have served to initiate generation after generation into the colonial paradigm. For many children in North America and elsewhere, the tale of Columbus is totemic; it introduces them not only to the concepts of "discovery" and the "New World," but also to the idea of history itself....Only some voices and perspectives, it is implied, resonate in the world. (p. 62)

Technology discourses as currently articulated in education are enactments of epistemic violence, translinguistic and Eurolingual, carriers of Eurocentric ideas, theories, and practices across the curricula. Manifest manners is demonstrated as Eurocentric ways of taking up the world seem to have become a universal, ubiquitous default position, and the ultimate place of legitimacy against which all other knowledge is measured and templated. Eurocentric educational discourses, and technology discourses, specifically, are western geographies that fix and constitute culture according to western criteria, and at the same time absent or erase Indigenous epistemologies and technologies.

Aboriginal Peoples, like other rhizomes and nomads (crabgrass, dandelions, Coyotes, and small 'c' coyotes) have been pulled up by their roots and expected to die. "A buried root. A nuisance people dig up and throw into the sun to wither. A globe of frail seeds that's indestructible" (Erdrich, 1993, p. 258). The biggest holocaust in history (100 million Aboriginal Peoples between 1492 and 1550) happened in North America and is still happening (Churchill, 1998; Cole, 2000a), another in Australia, in which 85%–95% of Aboriginal Peoples were eradicated through military strikes, being hunted down for bounties on their scalps, starvation, and biological warfare such as smallpox-infected blankets (Cole, 2000a). While the dominant culture has tried to eradicate these "nuisances" and their traditional knowings, it has been discovering some uses for their traditions, medicines, and technologies. Aboriginal knowings, stories, and artefacts are being appropriated, trivialized, trinketized, and marketed for healing western ills—for profit. On the plagiarism front they are being patented and copyrighted by (mostly) white academics and entrepreneurs. Aboriginal Peoples have been treated as *pre*historic untapped natural resources—*pre* meaning beyond Euro literacies and histories. Aboriginal ontologies, sensibilities, and relationships are lost in the marketplace. Spirit and survival and ceremony are reduced to New Age pecuniary and pilfery—Henry Wadsworth Longfellow's *The Song of Hiawatha*, Michael Blake's *Dances with Wolves*, Robert Bly's "wild man" in *Iron John*, Robert Bringhurst's *As Sharp as a Knife: The Classical Haida Mythtellers and Their World*, and Disney's *Pocahontas* (brown Barbie). Wannabes are the world's largest tribe. However, as Grillo (1998) writes, western perceptions of aboriginality can only be western:

> Intellectuals, technicians and artists in general consider that the terminology of modern Western culture is the only valid one....Academia has taught them that there is a single world and that it is the modern Western world; and they have taken pains to learn it well. But the reality is not like that; there are as many worlds as there are cultures. Therefore, whatever evaluation that can be made of the Andean world in terms that are foreign to it, simply does not concern it. (p. 128)

It is important to do more than merely communicate across a border to another culture, transiting the imaginary line of othernesses. How did the border get there in the first place, and how is it maintained? By whom?

Although postcolonial and minority critics have challenged the dominant politics of knowledge, postcolonial theories will never help Indigenous Peoples. What is needed is the unsettling and undoing of hierarchies so that all knowledges are treated equitably, rather than treating some as being 'less' equal.

> we are the mainstream   which is made up of tributaries
> my language and people are part of that stream   the tributaries are not greater or lesser than what they flow into
> (Cole & O'Riley, 2002, p. 147)

Western technology discourses not only have huge cultural and socioeconomic implications worldwide; they have devastating effects on the environment as currently being played out with global warming, the hole in the ozone, droughts, ice storms, El Niño, melting of ice caps, air pollution, toxic waste, poisoned rivers, lakes, and oceans, to name a few. Progress in the form of individual, corporate, inter/trans/national and global financial competition for profit is promoted, whereas cooperation, sharing and sustainable communities are downplayed. As Stephen Petrina (2000a) writes, technology education is located in a "liberal, political ecology and in effect, our conventional models—our practices—are not sustainable" (p. 208). Dominant discourses are about resourcing and desourcing, with people, forests, rivers, stones, and even sunlight becoming resources, quantized packages of economic jargon, a first step toward transforming them into growing profits for an ever wealthier and ever more anti-environmental elite. Considering the significant push for students to reproduce the "selfish gene" (Bowers, 2002) by learning to become good producers/consumers (tech ed) and virtual subjectivities (ed tech), and considering the ecological state of the earth, educators need to stop and take a breath in the seductive hyperstimulation of "technocapitalism" (Best & Kellner, 2001) so that we have time and space to evaluate and remap the interrelationships between environmental degradation and the "bourgeois consciousness" (Kroker & Weinstein, 1994) of the technology discourses we offer in schools.

A more critical and responsible conversation on technology is urgently needed. Technological literacy in schools needs to take on a whole new set of meanings, values, and configurations. Such a conversation requires articulation from a much more diverse epistemological community if the destruction enacted by western paradigms of representation and cultural reproduction is to be acknowledged, problematized, and addressed. If, as many curriculum documents suggest, education is to become a place *for all students*, and if female students and students from a diversity of cultures and ethnicities are to become more than ontological and epistemological optical illusions in technology classrooms, different ways of seeing and acting beyond the rhetorical gestures of gender and cultural inclusivity are crucial. Environmental concerns can no longer be tokenized, absented, ignored, or denied. I am arguing for a remapping of technology discourses to become respectful "mutual intercultural conversations" (Apffel-Marglin, 1998; Grillo, 1998) in which dynamic, multiple dimensionalities and tonalities come to the foreground, and where students become *actors* (active subjects) rather than (in)scripted learners (passive objects) of *pre*scribed knowledge constructs. I am committed to partnering with diverse knowledge communities, locally and globally, to revision technologies in ways that are more equitable, caring, and inclusive of all peoples, as well as environmentally sustainable.

One Woman's Story

> In the act of writing there's an attempt to make life something more than personal, to free life from what imprisons it. You write with the view of an unborn people that doesn't yet have a language. (Deleuze, 1995, p. 143)

I, too, write from the view of an unborn person and into a language that is not yet. *Technology, Culture, and Socioeconomics: A Rhizoanalysis of Educational Discourses* is an interruption of the flow of the prevailing technology discourses offered in education. This is one woman's uniquely contexted dimensionality connecting with other bodies, voices, and geographies to create a conversation, rather than conversion or conflation, of different technology stories. It is an explicitly geopolitical adventure, an effort to make room for "difference" (Deleuze, 1994a) in an era of revived neo-liberalism and global corporate capitalism marked by standardization, time and space compression, digital communication, global capital, unfettered development and consumerism, techno- and bioweapons of mass destruction, environmental degradation, millions of people unable to access health care, and people in the billions starving. This writing journey is an incitement to the "insurrection of subjugated knowledges" (Braidotti, 1994b) that co-exist with mainstream discourses but have been ignored in the recent reductionist moves to standardize curricula. It is not my intention to create a new hybrid or a successor technology discourse (add gender, culture, socioeconomics, environment, etc., and stir). I seek to encourage a *discourse of difference,* a more vivacious, tactile, and passionate engagement in a world increasingly being inscribed by, and compressed into, normalized discourses and anaesthetized virtual environments further intensifying the gulf between 'us' and 'them.'

This writing is largely (in)formed by research undertaken for my doctoral studies, though some of the footwork began with my master's thesis, *Contextualizing the Gendered and Industrial Bias of Technology Education* (1992), a Marxist feminist critique dealing primarily with gender inequity and corporate influences on technology curricula. The research undertaken for my doctoral studies took place at two sites. The initial and most extensive segment relates to technology education and was done with grades 11 and

12 technology education students and their teacher at a high school in British Columbia, Canada, whereas the educational technology segment was done with educational technology graduate students at a university in New Jersey, USA, where I was teaching at the time. The research required that I become itinerant, a sojourner without a permanent resting place, as well as an irritant. From a place of awkwardness and oblique angles, fulfilling the gap(s) between the terrain of technology education discourses and educational technology, I sought to become *otherwise* and *elsewhere*, manoeuvering through the perverse etymologies and fossilized landmarks that appear as landmines (languagemines) to me. *Elsewhere* and *otherwise* are not something or somewhere else, but among, within, and about each of us. They do not reside in a future time and place, but here, now. Doing this work required that I take on the role of double agent as I sought out different methodologies while troubling the practice of doing research itself (including my own). It required that I trouble the taken-for-granteds of western research methodology such as the notion of the 'right to know,' what and who is deemed to be data, the privileged position and authority of researcher to researched, and the (im)possibility of ethics within an academic frame of reference. It created a desire to experiment with different and hopefully less researcher-centred and more collective ways of doing data.

My interest in technology started long before I entered academia. In my journeying, I have scaled many plateaux. My theories of technology are intersected by a whole footsore, backache and weathering of lived experiences with, and knowledge of, technology in the real world. I bring to this conversation more than twenty years' experience in private industry and government in the areas of building design, construction, building inspection, labour relations, human rights, and occupational health and safety. Much of my work has been in areas considered nontraditional for women. As well, I have been a trade union activist. These experiences have provided me with valuable hands-on knowledge of, and experience with, the diversity and complexity of technologies, including their gender, cultural, socioeconomic, and environmental implications in the public and private spheres and the spaces between.

I am one of the very few women who have entered the male domain of technology education. When I went into industrial education (the former name of technology education) in 1988, there were approximately 1,100 industrial education teachers in British Columbia of whom only five were female—roughly 99.5% of industrial education teachers were male. All of the full-time instructors who taught the technical component and the university professor who taught the academic component of the teacher education programme were, and still are, white males. Fifteen years later, in spite of considerable efforts by females, and males who support equity and diversity, the scene remains unchanged (Braundy, O'Riley, & Petrina, 2000). Further, as Mary Bryson and Suzanne de Castell's (1996) research indicates, British Columbia Ministry of Education gender equity policies have done little to improve gender inequity in the student population:

> The spread of technology-intensive areas in the school curriculum in which boys predominate is pervasive, with the notable exception of cooking and clothing and textiles courses. This finding has remained essentially unaltered throughout the duration of an explicit B.C. Ministry of Education "gender equity" policy. In other words, the situation of under-representation and disciplinary "ghettoization": for girls in B.C. public school has not improved over the last ten years. (p. 5)

My understandings and experiences are on the margins of the overwhelming majority of technology educators' understandings and concerns, and most times they are right off their gender, culture, socioeconomic, and environment radar/sonar. Rather than seeing this as deficit positioning, I celebrate this as a dynamic position where I can inhabit and explore different worlds both within and beyond the currently acknowledged maps of technology education. From this standpoint, this particular plateau, I fix my template and micro-lenses, zooming in and out, contexting, reconstituting, surveying, and taking time to breathe, feel, remember. One gender is being under-represented by a factor of a hundred—and it's not males.

My knowledge and experience of technology discourses crosses international borders. I have taught technology education at universities in Canada and New Zealand, and educational technology at two universities in the United States, at the undergraduate and post-baccalaureate levels, and graduate levels. I have been an invited scholar at Deakin University in Melbourne,

Australia, where I explored the possibilities of integrating technology education with environmental education. Funded by the British High Commission, I have met with technology educators and students at universities and colleges in the United Kingdom. The *Design Technology Curriculum* there has gone through significant, though equally problematic revisioning. Technological capability, rather than technological literacy, is the preferred term. In the United Kingdom, home economics and art education were incorporated within industrial arts, however, reshaping them such that most of their former curricular context and practices were disengaged from the domestic sphere while appropriating textiles and foods for the design and making of mainly consumer products.

My understandings and experiences go beyond western frameworks and protocols. In New Zealand, the Maori have considerable influence in education because of the Treaty of Waitangi. In consideration of this cultural intercourse, while teaching there I designed and taught my courses seeking input, guidance, and participation of members of the Maori (and Pacific Islander) communities so that mainstream and indigenous knowings were both foregrounded. My partner, Dr. Peter Cole, who is In-SHUCK-ch/Lower Stl'atl'imx (British Columbia) and professor of Aboriginal Education at the University of Victoria, and I were invited to contribute to the new Maori technology education curriculum. Maori curricula to that point had been little more than translations into the Maori language of Eurocentric curricula. Rather than repeating this form of cultural assimilation and genocide, *Technology in the New Zealand Curriculum* was reshaped by Maori educators into *Hangarau: i roto i te Marautanga o Aotearoa,* a curriculum based as much as possible within the political constraints of the day on Maori spirituality, knowledges, and technologies to be taught in Maori schools by Maori educators.

Through my participation in my partner's community, learning more about my Mohawk heritage, and with colleagues from Kenya, Australia, New Zealand, Belize, Peru, Colombia, Sudan, Mexico, the United States, and Canada, I am (re)learning ways of being in the world that are neither theoretical nor linguistic, but are different conversations. This involves what Eduardo Fernandez Grillo (1998) writes of as a reciprocal "nurturing and being nurtured," a conversation of humans, plants, soils, waters, animals, climates, and so on—quite foreign to anything I had learned in my "formal" education, in particular the western notions of individualism, competition, and humans as being superior to all other living things. Always the objective is subsumed, subtended by the subject. I am deeply affected by these conversations.

Journal entry, November 1991:

> I pause   and wonder
> about my own aboriginal ancestry   geography
> about my mohawk and french grandmother
> a place of mainly silence in our family
> except for a short stop   at the reserve on the way
> to visit my irish and french relations in quebec
> I pause   and wonder
> about Coyote   emerging from
> and surviving my general examination
> in the midst of talk
> of cyborgian imagery in schools
> in which Coyote
> was being technologized into a cyborg trickster
> is my own geography at this time such a coincidence
> the pacific northwest
> where the weather is ever-changing   unpredictable
> where aboriginal peoples are gaining   strength
> is it a coincidence that the small 'c' coyote is resisting
> all human endeavours to eradicate her
> moving   into urban areas
> including the endowment lands
> at the university of british columbia
> not to mention parking lots
> around simon fraser university
> named after simon the 'discoverer'
>   paddle   paddle
> perhaps they want to move   trickster
> discourse into the university   the place
> of one true story   but
> that one got away

The understandings and experiences of technology that resonate most intimately in my own life do not come from academia or the workplace, but from living in the world. I learned very young the technologies of the home—caring for my younger brother and two younger sisters, sewing diapers, making clothes, creating meals out of little more than imagination. I learned when and how to collect sap, what berries and mushrooms to pick, how to garden, how to fish, how to read animals tracks in the snow, what springs to drink from, when the Skootamata River was thick enough to skate on, and how to swim and canoe. I made myself a drafting board and taught myself how to do architectural drafting from library books because I did not have the opportunity to gain a post-secondary education. Later in life, I designed and built my own home. These are *technologies of nurturance, sustainability, and survival*.

Writing Plateaux

Deterritorializing the terrain of technology discourses in education is not a simple task. There are embankments of petrified sedimentations and deeply pocketed fortifications of already-mapped territories, as well as the complexities of gender, culture, socio-economics, and environment. Seeking possibilities beyond the technoterritorial maps of standardized technology discourses, as well as (un)folding the hypertexts and hyperrealities of educational technology, requires a different languaging, communicating, and strategizing. How is it possible to open technology discourses to different stories, the unsaid, the unthought, the ineffable? How might I begin to engage with the processes, dynamics, and rhythms that co-exist within the hegemonic technology discourses but have been dismissed or silenced because they neither fit technocratic capitalist agendas nor other Eurocentric cultural frameworks. Where might I begin to map an *elsewhere* and *otherwise* without relying on grids, isobars, fronts, and lows? From what projections and models do I work? How often do you see a polar projection used in looking at the world, or a map, with Africa or New Zealand as the focal/global centre?

A stutterer himself, Gilles Deleuze (1994b) writes of stuttering as a performative language making, a merging of language and speech, a poetic speech. Within s-s-s-stuttering there is space for both sounds and silents/s s   pace   s.

> Stuttering no longer affects preexisiting words, but, rather, itself ushers in the words that it affects...the words do not exist independently of the stutterer, which selects and links them together.
>
> It is no longer the individual who stutters in his speech, it is the writer who *stutters in the language system (langue)*: he causes language as such to stutter. (p. 23)

In *A Thousand Plateaus: Capitalism & Schizophrenia*, Gilles Deleuze and Félix Guattari (1987), wrote plateaux rather than chapters as s-s-s-stuttering textual practice.

> We are writing this book as a rhizome. It is composed of plateaus. We have given it a circular form, but not for laughs. Each morning we would wake up, and each of us would ask himself what plateau he was going to tackle, writing five lines here, ten lines there. We had hallucinatory experiences, we watched lines leave one plateau and proceed to another like columns of tiny ants. We made circles of convergence. Each plateau can be read starting anywhere and can be related to any other plateau. (p. 22)

For Deleuze and Guattari, chapters have culmination and termination points; however, writing plateaus "abandons any semblance of narrative or argument exposition in favour of random, perspectival juxtaposition of chapters, or 'plateaus' comprised of complex conceptual flows" (Best & Kellner, 1991, p. 98). Cole (2002) adds a cultural dimensionality that is not part of Deleuze and Guattari's conversation:

> the idea of chapter   is anathema to who I am
> as an indigenous person
> it implies western order as 'the' legitimate shaper
> of discourse
> the universe being ordered into rationally constructed geometries
> precluding enthalpy to be the prescribed
> means of navigating
> rather than entropy   devalidating our own symbolic
> sense of ourselves
> perceptions of our perceptions   making us take up
> the tools of the settlers (p. 448)

Each plateau is a different stuttering—a resonance, a vibration toward finding and creating holes in enclosed narratives. Each is a throw of the dice (Nietzsche, 1961). Plateaux are composed of segments of writing that hold together disparate elements, combinations of concepts that "bring an activity or thought to a pitch of intensity that is not automatically dissipated in a climax leading to a state of rest" (Massumi, 1992, p. 7). The dynamic afterimages and sounds can become reanimated or combined with other activities creating a nonhomogeneous texting of any number of conjunctive possibilities—a thousand tiny folds, micro-perceptions. Plateaux transversally implicate an array of diverse subjects, times, and disciplines. They are places of connection and transition, between mountains and riverbeds, places of erosion and new growth, hoodoos, mesas, soil becoming silt, plant, animal in other geographies, times, relation(ships).

I enter into this writing journey at the borders, the frontiers, of my knowings and practices; trembling, stumbling, s-s-s-stuttering within and without the dominant technology discourses. This book is a series of stutterings, a series of plateaux, of resonances and vibrations, oscillations, to encourage more complex, contingent, and indeterminate theories and practices. Each plateau is an inchoate and alternative mapping, a cartographic gesture to cause the hegemonic languaging of technology "to cry, to make it stutter, mumble, or whisper" (Deleuze, 1994b, p. 25). Geographically, topographically, epistemologically, methodologically, each plateau becomes an isthmus, a connector. I write these plateaux as

> an archipelago—a smattering of seemingly unconnected isolated epistemo-*geographies* which are identified not by their submarine and occulted connections with one another, but by their surface features, such as being other than mainland, extra-continental, being surrounded by water (disconnected) islands, like understandings, have to do with levels of awareness, tidal shifts, gravitation, (heavenly) bodies in relation, points of view. If the sea level went down sufficiently, the (conceptual) archipelago would become one island or even part of the mainland, a peninsula. (Cole, 1996, p. 4)

The story changes as I change or as I am layered by my experiences. I seek to include nonvisual metaphors to companion plant—the heard/unheard, felt/unfelt, tasted/untasted, smelled/unsmelled—to escape contemporary western culture's addiction to the visual. I am not unaware of the trap of using paired perceptivities, including the prefix 'un-' as an antonymic gesture which polarizes the mind as it makes efforts to divide ideas into camps or cold frames as it journeys through the dynamic templates of grammar and usage. I do not seek to binarize. I speak of pairs, not as complete units, but as partners sharing a broader epistemological journey with other co-journeyers.

Plateaux are very familiar places for Coyote, a trickster to Aboriginal Peoples. Plateaux are her/his natural habitat, so s/he joins the conversation when s/he feels her/his insight is required. Coyote has survived manifest manners for over five hundred years so is not coincidental to this writing journey into the predominantly western terrain of technology discourses in education. Coyote has weathered/whethered all kinds of turbulences from cultural and biological genocide to imperial imaginings. Somehow she always manages to land on all four paws. Coyote insisted on insinuating her/him/self into my research and my doctoral dissertation de- and re-scripting my thoughts and vocabulary, not to mention prolonging/lengthening the writing process. Without prior notice s/he dropped in and out of the conversations I had with the co-researchers and the theorists uprooting and shapeshifting technology discourses, as well as the terrain of my writing. Every now and then in order to understand the tricksterisms, I use a CPI (Coyote Positioning Instrument) that allows me to switch off the purely rational parts of myself so I can become open to (her/his) other/wise. Peter Cole, a trickster himself, prompts Raven and Coyote, tricksters of the Pacific Northwest to share their voices within this text. Coyote's appearances are sometimes as a four-legged and Raven's as a wingéd one. Sometimes they appear in human form, often as/in nature.

This book is not an enclosed storytelling nor an elaborate system of textual defense moving toward a gripping conclusion; rather it is a radical (actually, rhizomatic) writing journey mixing and juxtaposing styles, genres, theories, and practices—always in a state of "becoming" (Deleuze & Guattari, 1987). I strive to honour the words I have borrowed from other writers by allowing them to speak for themselves as much as possible. As Peter Cole (2000a) suggests, a poem, itself, is a translation, an interpretation. In the case of Deleuze and Guattari, whose work I make affiliations with throughout this book, their work is already translated from French to English. How can I translate an already once removed translation, an interpretation of a translation? Writing Deleuze and Guattari is not writing *about* Deleuze and Guattari. My connections with their words are merely my connections. I do not have any illusions of making correct or authoritative connections. I seek potentialities in the segments of their writing that gesture to me in my effort to free life from the dominant technology discourses in education. Providing the reader with more than writ rote, perhaps the cited authors can play a more central and performative role, and the reader can become a part of the conversation by making their own connections.

As I traverse through and beyond dominant technology discourses, technology students and their teacher, educational technology graduate students, a colleague from Kenya, together with western and indigenous theorists, join me. We converge, diverge, and interverge, taking different paths and contours, making new/old connections, changing our angles of perception to see from other projections, letting go of conventional wisdom and willful ignorance. As we gather our thoughts and try to stuff them into chapters, plateaux (or mesas depending on Coyote's sense of humour), they leak out, disappear, and reappear in other places and in other forms, shapeshifting my intentions. Just like real life. This writing is indeed partial, fluid, fragmentary, and ambiguous, the words carried on the landscape of the wind, water, grasses, and trees, sometimes to the sounds of Coyote and Raven. The meanings and understandings are limited only by y/our own imagination.

Topographical Legend

Re: mapping positions the theoretical geography for the journeys of this text introducing "rhizomatics" (Deleuze & Guattari, 1987), "nomadics" (Braidotti, 1994a, 2002; Deleuze & Guattari, 1987), "trickster discourse" and "narrative chance" (Vizenor, 1993), as well as "chance operations" and "poethics" (Cage, 1994) as a s-s-s-stuttering cartographic gesture to remap technology discourses. *Mesa Morphing Methodology* situates the methodological positionings of the study. Research methodology is framed, unframed, (in)validated, and teased into new lines of flight invoking a *meth-*

odology of difference which makes conjunctions with rhizomes, tricksters, and chance operations. *Siting Tech Ed* examines the historical roots of technology education as industrial education, as well as the imbrication of technology discourses with global corporate and military technocapitalism. *Shapeshifting Tech Ed* is an intermezzo, an intercultural rhizo-dance, a disruptive move to open the technology conversation in education to stories that are beyond, or have fallen right off the edges of western maps, in particular feminist, antiracist, anticolonial, indigenous, and environmental stories. *Virtual(ly) Ed Tech* is a theoretical space where real and virtual environments converge, digress, and interpose in relation to the new politics of alliances formed in the promotion of computer and multimedia technologies in education. Posthumans and cyborgs abound. *A Dataplay* is a performative space, a rhizoanalysis of virtual education coscripted with graduate students as a dataplay in which we all become characters, including the theorists. The dataplay acts as data and analysis, the data arising initially from the educational technology teachers' journal writing about teaching with computer and multimedia technologies. It is a mi-jeté, a space to pause and be still or fouetté with the dervish, a spinnaker of multiple engagement. This writing journey comes to a terminus with *Joining Landscape and Epistemologies* which folds back to the previous plateaux as a synthanalysis and imagining of potentialities for technology discourses in education to become more equitable, socially and culturally just, and environmentally responsible conversations.

Re: Mapping

> I want to draw a map, so to speak, of a critical geography and use that map to open as much space for discovery, intellectual adventure, and close exploration without the mandate for conquest.
> —Toni Morrison, *Playing in the Dark*

> The map of the world that we carry within ourselves would do well to include the boundaries of its own geography. If there is a geographic determinism of the world, it lies in how we have learned to imagine distance and difference.
> —John Willinsky, *Learning to Divide the World*

On a precipice in an unknown territory, I empty my backpack and re-explore possible chartings and tools for the theoretical geography of this journey. I listen to the sounds of the birds, the four leggéds, the rushing water, the wind in the trees, the rhythm of the earth, and my own breath as I try to locate my geo/somato/metapositioning(s) and situate the parameters and limit(ation)s of my own experiences and knowings in the world. As I sort through my tools, supplies, maps, survival strategies, and emergency procedures for remapping of a different terrain for technology discourses in education, I consider other possibilities, always leaving room for those yet to come. I pause, await inspiration.

I unfold, shake out, and refold critical and feminist theories, as well as poststructural and 'post'/anti/colonial theories. I realize, in airing out and repacking, that feminist and critical theories have done much to transform understandings of patriarchy and capitalism, while poststructural theories have offered a way to open the rhetoric of universal technology discourses beyond mirroring (reflection), toward a more refractive and diffusive engagement.

These provide a "theoretical vocabulary and a language of decolonizing for piercing the closed horizons of technology, and for listening intently to the 'intimations of deprival' in the midst of the celebratory ruins of the American way," as well as "resistance strateg[ies] for living in a culture tattooed by digital reality" (Kroker, 1992, p. 165). Language becomes a virus (Anderson, 1994) creating potential to disrupt and contaminate the structures and practices of the *techno*logical one true story, to enact more noninnocent (rather than value-neutral) *geo*logical storytelling practices—not just the heard but also stories from/of the land. Poststructural theories s-s-s-stutter; they are speaking in tongues as "writing focuses on the outer flow of speech, seeking not the thought that 'underlies' speech, but the thought that is speech" (Tyler, quoted in Vizenor, 1993, p. 4) Coyote howls. Full moon rises. The wind is up.

Rhizomatics

John Willinsky (1998) writes that the legacy of imperialism in the West is that we are "schooled in differences" and, I add, to become indifferent. We are taught how to divide the world and to construct borderlines of discrimination and difference "between civilized and primitive, West and East, first and third worlds, [fourth worlds, other and not-other]...to the disadvantage of so many people" (pp. 1–2). Difference is constructed as other, as negative. Exotic. How might it be possible to reterritorialize technology discourses, which are increasingly devoted to integrated world capitalism, turning students into future compliant, docile *techno*thinking *techno*subjects ready for their place in the global corporatocracy? How might it be possible to remap the *order-words* with stories that circulate both within and beyond the dominant borders into a different geography with different languages, thoughts, subjectivities? How might students be able to hear their own cries and laughter, the cries and laughter of others, the murmurs of the earth? Is it possible to find stillness and quiet amid the noise and hyperactivity, so that other stories out there and out of sight of the western horizon might be heard, acknowledged, included?

The work of Gilles Deleuze and Félix Guattari is a radical politics to subvert the normalizing theoretical and institutional barriers and codes of both psychoanalysis and capitalism. Their work is particularly relevant to remapping technology discourses as they become more controlled and standardized. Deleuze and Guattari (1987) are especially concerned with the growth of fascism, not only in political movements, but also the "microfascisms" within each of us, the "fascisms that cause us to love power, to desire the very thing that dominates and exploits us" (p. xiii). They refer to the social apparatuses within the dynamics of capitalist economy as "machines" that record, channel, and regulate the coded flows of the "body of the earth...the body of the despot...and the body of capital"—machines "because their operations are not simply random; they are coded, or, rather, are loci where coding forms and maintains itself" (Lingis, 1994, p. 291).

> Deleuze & Guattari call attention to the problem of creative and vital existence in a global capitalism predicated on the narcoticization and robotization of its subjects. They emphasize the importance of combatting the ('paranoiac') personality type that requires rigid centredness, authority, stability, and obedience, the kind of subjects that cannot tolerate difference of others and march readily in fascist movements. (Best & Kellner, 1991, p. 105)

Their work offers critical analytic tools to loosen, untangle, and affirm life and lives from the narcoticization and robotization induced through the circuitry of technology discourses.

In *Difference & Repetition*, Deleuze (1994a) analyzes what he refers to as "capitalist axiomatization" in which the subject is folded inside from an outside through repetition and discipline, the subject is decoded for recoding and reforming into identity to coincide with capital and surplus value. Similar desires for recoding and reforming students to become human resources for global capital permeate contemporary technology discourses. Michel Foucault (1979) refers to such folding of the subject into the inside by the dominant culture's codings as "technologies of normalization." He argues that it is within the spaces of the shifting relations of the power/knowledge apparatuses where people become re-identified and recoded. Such sociocultural mapping and surveillance transform people into objects of an exterior gaze and subjects of what Michel Foucault writes of as an "interiorization of the gaze" and "technologies of self." Foucault provides the example of Jeremy Bentham's Panopticon or Inspection House, manifest in the form of a French prison. Everyone and everything becomes a part of the surveillance, the gaze, including the gazer. With the events of September 11, 2001, in New York City and Washington, DC, and the newer and more insidious legalized surveillance by police, military, and paramilitary organizations, *re*-revisioning technology discourses in education is all the more urgent. Educators need to place on the table a critical conversation on technology that includes new military bio- and surveillance technologies, as well as a re-consideration of the implications of normalizing student bodies to take their place in the New World Order, Inc. Deleuze (1995) cautions that the disciplinary societies Foucault wrote about are stealthily becoming "control societies." This development is evidenced in schools through increased standardization—hardening of the categories—of technology discourses. Curriculum becomes code (Robins & Webster, 1989), students become technically calibrated and narcoticized "pharma-codependents" (Ronell, 1993) to fit into a culture of compliance. Technological literacy is executed as the reproduction of "commodity bodies" (Massumi, 1987) isomorphing to capital as "connoisseurs" and "virtuosos of the code" (Foster, 1985) of technocapitalism; students (re)formed into soldiers of sameness.

Difference in education is not seen as something to celebrate and animate; rather what is not viewed as the norm is seen as negative, something to vanquish or subordinate, contain, control by reducing difference to the Same. For Deleuze (1994a), perpetual displacement of difference "restores bare, mechanical and stereotypical repetitions, within and without us" from which we extract "little differences, variations and modification....Repetitions repeat themselves, while *the differenciator differenciates* itself" (p. 247) working rhizomatically to find life and breath external to the conforming standardizations. This journey is an attempt to differenciate, to extract little differences, variations, and modifications from the bare, mechanical, and stereotypical repetitions of technology discourses. I look for "holey spaces" in the "apparatus of capture" (Deleuze & Guattari, 1987) of the textual and material practices of technology discourses that fuse bodies, geographies, space, and time into the grids of cybertechnology, patriarchy, and global corporatocracy. My desire is that these differenciations, becomings, s-s-s-stutterings, affirm difference by occupying the order words, inventing a different space-time, and potentially and vitally disrupting the official representations of technology.

Deleuze and Guattari offer the concept of "rhizome" as a cartographic gesture of deterritorialization in contradistinction to what they refer to as western "arborescent thought," which is organized systematically and hierarchically as branches of knowledge grounded in firm foundations. While arborescent thought seeks to colonize rhizomes and to turn them into deeply rooted structures, rhizomes differenciate:

> The rhizome is altogether different, a map and not a tracing. Make a map, not a tracing....What distinguishes the map from the tracing is that it is entirely oriented toward an experimentation in contact with the real....The map is open and connectable in all of its dimensions; it is detachable, reversible, susceptible to constant modification. It can be torn, reversed, adapted to any kind of mounting, reworked by an individual, group, or social formation. It can be drawn on a wall, conceived of as a work of art, constructed as a political action or a meditation...has multiple entryways, as opposed to the tracing, which always comes back "to the same." The map has to do with performance, whereas the tracing always involves alleged "competence." (pp. 12–13)

Rhizomes are not roots, but underground stems. They affirm what is excluded from western thought and reintroduce reality as dynamic, heterogeneous, and nondichotomous; they implicate rather than replicate; they propagate, displace, join, circle back, fold. Emphasizing the materiality of desire, rhizomes like crabgrass, ants, wolf packs, and children, de- and reterritorialize space. Rhizomatic lines have no beginning or end; they are always in the process of *becoming*. Deleuze and Guattari write of three types of lines: *molar*, which fix and normalize identities within social institutions; *molecular*, which are the cracks in the rigidity of the molar; and *lines of flight*, "where cracks become ruptures and the subject is shattered in a process of becoming multiple" (Best & Kellner, 1991, p. 100). As such, multiplicities are not created as multiples of the Same, thus interrupting attempts at overcoding. Such a multiplicity is a syncretization, changing territorialities and positionalities, much like Raven and Coyote, with lines of flight folding back on its rhizome-multiplicity to become one of its dimensionalities, *regenerating* its potential of further becoming.

Several feminists have been taking up the rhizome in their work. For Elizabeth Grosz (1994), rhizomatics is a form of pragmatics concerned with what can be done. For her, rhizomatics "provide a powerful ally and theoretical resource for feminist challenges to the domination of philosophical paradigms, methods, and presumptions that have governed the history of western thought and have perpetuated, rationalized, and legitimated erasure of women and women's contributions from cultural, sexual, and theoretical life" (p. 190). Grosz enters into the rhizomatic project articulated by Deleuze and Guattari as an exploration and navigation of feminist conjunctions toward nomadic thought and nomadic subjectivity. She is particularly interested in surfacing the question of the "centrality of ethics, of the encounter of otherness" (p. 196), rather than constructing prescriptive moral imperatives. Rosi Braidotti (1994b) considers rhizomatics as a way to rethink alterity and otherness. Dorothea Olkowski (1994) views rhizomes as *active* forces that operate by means of self-affirmation, whereas *reactive* forces deny the other.

Working rhizomatically "there may be some surprises in store in the form of upsurges of young people, of women, that become possible simply because certain restrictions are removed (with 'untechnocratizable' consequences)" (Deleuze, 1995, p. 172). Rhizomes re-route the terrain, its tracks, and narratives that have been covered, inhumed, and otherwise disestablished through oligarchy in its many guises. The botanical nature of the rhizome figuration blurs the boundary between human and nature, with becoming as "ecosophy" and "points aléatoire" (Deleuze & Guattari, 1987), inclusive disjunctions, sensibly needed for understanding between all living things. Rhizomes are desire to live, and to be engaged in the world. Heliotropism. Geotropism. Both figuring and grounding. Rhizoanalysis is fluid, flexible, conjunctive, regenerating, and fun—not a place of dry linear intellectualization.

"Nomadic thought" is a form of rhizomatics that breaks with "State thought" causing it to s-s-stutter (Deleuze & Guattari,

1987). While State thought or "analogical thought starts from an isolated individual considered to be typical, and ends in a category coherent enough to take its rightful place in a preexisting system of good/common sense" (Massumi, 1992, p. 99), nomadic thought rides difference. "Rather than analyzing the world into discrete components, reducing their manyness to the One of identity, and ordering them by rank, it sums up a set of disparate circumstances in a shattering blow" (Massumi, 1987, p. xiii). Nomadic thought is becoming-bodily-thought, unhinging habitual and reactive thinking, regularity and normalized inscriptions. It grows from the middle, the cracks, the voids, the hyphens, the slashes, and the outcrops. It is in relation. Nomadic thought is an undoing, which pulls the door open on analogy, not by overturning habit, molarity, and reactivity, but by remapping a different space. Making new tracks, nomadic thought cherishes derelict spaces and holes in habits, and it maps a whole new virtual landscape featuring otherworldly affects, always marginal and transversal. It acts to blur boundaries and activate metaphors to become figurations *on the ground*. Other bodies and life spaces emerge.

Nomads traverse territory; they know the land, follow customary routes. They do not own or possess, but *inhabit* points, paths, and land. Similar to the First Peoples of this hemisphere, they know where they can find water and food and where to make shelters. Their routes are not fixed or in closed space; rather they are both the river and the tributaries that flow into it—which make up the mainstream. The life of the nomad is the intermezzo, yet intermezzo is integral, never merely an add-on. Nomads are not simply migrants; they speak the language *of* the land—not *logos*, but *nomos*. Nomads are not technologically primitive (Cole, 2000b; Deleuze & Guattari, 1987). They know how to liberate difference, provide new models, disorganize, and decode State thought and normalized subjectivity, and experiment with creativity to become or remain non- or antifascist. Nomads have infinite patience; they know how to wait; they appreciate the importance of silence—silence not as absence of sound, but the fullness of it. Becoming nomad is giving up a place that is safe, that is home, redefining what home is (not). For this journey, this means giving up the safety of universals and standards, the taken-for-granteds of hegemonic technology discourses.

Rosi Braidotti (1994a) suggests that to animate a nomadic subjectivity requires a "qualitative leap of the feminist political imagination" (p. 3) to create a figurative style of thinking, which is a politically informed way to "think differently about the subject, to invent new frameworks, new images, new modes of thought" (p. 1).

> The cartography of the...embodied subject, just like Foucault's diagrams of power, is always already the trace of what no longer is the case. As such it needs to be started all over again, constantly. In this repetition of the cartographic gesture there lies the potential for opening up new angles of vision, new itineraries. Nomadism is therefore neither a rhetorical gesture nor a mere figure of speech, but a political and epistemological necessity for critical theory at the end of this century. (p. 182)

Nomadic subjectivity starts with thought rooted/rhizomed in the body. The new nomadism advanced by Braidotti is not simply a matter of willful practice; it requests working through our history, our representations, and the storylines we live with/in. I suggest that nomadic subjectivity can be about more than the new; it can also be a way of regenerating knowings we already have; knowings that have been submerged in the swell and spume of Eurocentric thought and (re)activity—women's knowings, Indigenous knowings, the knowings students already have, as well as spiritual knowings that are downplayed in the West's ravenous quest for material goods and virtuality.

Another form of rhizome articulated by Deleuze and Guattari is their concept of "the minor" as one way to resist, exceed, and displace what Hal Foster (1985) refers to as the "monopoly of the code." The minor is a cultural practice that is in excess of the differential logic of the code. It is "an intensive, often vernacular use of language form which disrupts its official or institutional functions" (p. 177). The minor is not inert, disappearing behind or into the codes waiting only to be rewritten or read. Moreover, it does not want to (who/how does someone speak for 'it'?) become an official language or romanticize the marginal or individual; rather it is a "collective arrangement of utterances" (Bensmaia, 1994). Of significance to this remapping project is that a "minor literature is not the literature of a minor language but the literature a minority makes in a major language" (Deleuze & Guattari, 1987, p. 16).

> It is not a matter of opposing "reality" (which one?) to myth, but, on the contrary, given the existing circumstances, of extracting from the myth a "lived actual" that would make it possible to account for the impossibility of living in the conditions that people have inherited. (Bensmaia, 1994, p. 224)

It is finding a way out of the labyrinth of the majority language, which, in this case, is the material textual practices of technology discourses in education. Rather than paying allegiance to universals and standardization, my desire is to minorize technology discourses, trouble, destabilize their historical-lessness and context-lessness, which contribute to the division of the 'West' and 'the rest' through their instrumental rationalism and technification of the world. The task is not simply mixing or adding up minor languages, but causing the language to flee, to grow from the middle(s), placing it in a state of perpetual and shifting equilibrium.

> It is when the language system overstrains itself that it begins to stutter, to murmur, or to mumble, then the entire language reaches the limit that sketches the outside and confronts silence. When the language system is so much strained, language suffers a pressure that delivers it to silence. (Deleuze, 1994b, p. 28)

Minor languages present uncompleted pasts repressed by capitalism and colonization, and they intensify these contradictions in the present. As Hal Foster (1985) suggests, minorizing majority discourse connects "the buried...the disqualified (the minor) and the yet-to-come (utopian or better than desired) in concerted cultural practices" (p. 179). Minorizing discourse can deterritorialize and remap a missing terrain, people, and signs. The geography and the people are not missing, except in the majority language. First Peoples have had to learn how to minorize the majority language in the reclaiming of their land and their culture through the revival of their traditional oral languages that have been whited out, laundered by the dominant culture.

    I encourage my undergraduate and graduate students to use their own voice for their writing assignments, rather than a borrowed one, rather than the one they might think I want to hear, including using their own (other) languages where there is no equivalence in English. Last winter, a Japanese student in my *Language, Culture, and Education* graduate course came running down the hall to tell me that she had never written poetry before and decided to write her final essay for the course in a poetic voice using some of her Japanese language. She was thrilled at how she could feel her writing flow through her as it became more intimately connected to what she wanted to express on paper. In New Zealand, many Maori words are making their way into the everyday speech, joining the English language with Maori knowings and protocols, and the land on which both the Maori and Pakeha (settlers) live.

As exciting as Deleuze and Guattari's politics of difference is, I have some similar concerns as those raised below by Steven Best and Douglas Kellner (1991). Their first concern is that collective struggle and possibilities for large-scale social transformation (mainly against technocapitalism) get lost in microanalysis and politics, "a postmodern replay of the aestheticist tradition of modernity...seeking refuge in art, the body, and highly individualized modes of being" (p. 109). Deleuze (1995) writes "[w]hat we are interested in, you see, are modes of individuation" (p. 26). Best and Kellner believe that issues of intersubjectivity and social relations become undertheorized in the individuality of becoming. They are also concerned with the productivist mode of Deleuze and Guattari's concept of desire.

> For Deleuze and Guattari, desire is neither inherently good nor bad, only dynamic and productive; desiring machines can travel along the path of becoming-revolutionary as well as becoming-fascist; lines of escape can turn into liberation or destruction. (p. 105)

Desire for Deleuze and Guattari is a radical departure from the Lacanian desire for Other to fill our perceived lack; rather it is always in a state of becoming, affirming of life. Western education would be a very different conversation if Deleuze and Guattari's notion of desire were taken up rather than the current practices of placing so much effort into maintaining a divide between us and them. Best and Kellner question how the "Deleuzo-Guattarian 'ethic'...breaks from capitalist and consumerist behaviour" (p.

107), and argue for intersubjectivity and a politics of alliances at both micro- and macrolevels. For me, such a politics also lives in the liminal spaces between and outside of the micro- and macrolevels, distinctions most often associated with critical and Marxist theories.

Best and Kellner's concerns resonate with my own disquiet about the unequivocal emphasis on "needs and wants" in education that create a desire in students to become producers and consumers. Both technology discourses and curriculum inquiry are about production of more, better, and new: one produces new commodities; the other produces new information. Verena Andermatt Conley (1993) expresses her concern with the appropriation of *becoming* by global technocapitalism for destructive ends.

> Next to exhorting subjects, in a minuscule semantic shift, to remain flexible, it mirrors another, false becoming, one of temporal obsolescence, hence new markets....In a market economy, it has shifted toward destruction and the staggering production of unusable trash. (p. 85)

Conley maintains that under "the guise of *fake becoming*, that is, of a betterment and irreversible improvement of reality used for the marketing of products, capitalism thrusts people forward while engaging them in a deadly race in which profit is the only motive for advancement" (p. 82). This fake becoming masks the perpetuation of colonialism and colonization as it mobilizes those who have created a greater divide between those who have and those who have not, "exacerbating local ecological struggles anywhere and at once, all over the globe" (p. 85).

Rhizomatics Meets Trickster Discourse

Trickster discourse is a minorizing discourse that has been around long before Deleuze and Guattari's conceptualization of "the minor," and it is an important dimension of the culture of the First Peoples of North America. According to Gerald Vizenor (1993), trickster discourse creates "narrative chance, comic holotropes and dissident narratives," offering potential for remapping, freeing our imagination so that it can do "pleasurable misreadings" and rewriting of *what counts as technology*. Trickster discourse is a form of postmodern storytelling, *Canis rhizomaticus*, yet it has been around much longer than modernism and its posts. Trickster discourse has different in/sights/sites from the majority discourse, an at once serious and comic discourse, which is relational, a collage, a pastiche, a montage, of utterances and practices that deny completion for reintegration.

> Serious attention to cultural hyperrealities is an invitation to trickster discourse, an imaginative liberation in comic narratives: the trickster is postmodern. (Vizenor, 1993, p. 9)

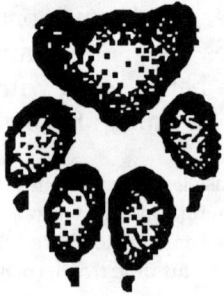

> The trickster is "within language" and not a neutral instrument that reveals codes and structural harmonies. The trickster is a sign and a patent language game in a narrative discourse; science is language closure, a monologue in theoretical contention. (p. 194)

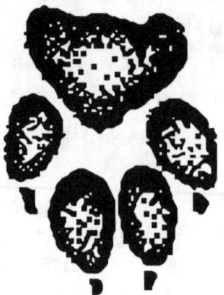

> The trickster is not a structural code or an invitation to the arcane. The trickster is a comic sign not a trope to power in social science. (p. 192)

Orthodox science demands one true story, one that is objective, valid. Wild knowledge has no place in social science monologues; it escapes and exceeds capturing (for consumption and analysis).

> nanabuzho that crazy one s/he dances and moves
> and jives and shadows
> and does all kinds of verb things
> the english language has no idea about
> s/he's a coyote raven transformer
> wild and crazy spirit wrestler that one (Cole, 2000b, p. 3)

Trickster discourse is an aeolian harp and an animated landscape, the horizons forever in motion. Trickster Coyotes and coyotes are weatherers/whetherers and need a lot of space, not the closed and sterile environments of hyperreality. Hyperreality talks with hyperreality, not with the land, nor the people, whereas Trickster, whether it be Coyote or Raven or Nanabuzho, speaks to the imagination, speaks with anyone who will listen, and listens to anyone who wishes to speak.

> The best listeners were shadows, animals, birds, and humans, because their shadows once shared the same stories. [Bagese] said there were tricksters in our voices and natural sounds, tricksters who remembered the scenes, the wild visions in the shadows of the words. She warned me that even the most honored lectures were dead voices, that shadows were dead recitations. She said written words were the burial grounds of shadows. The tricksters in the word are seen in the ear not the eye. (Vizenor, 1992, p. 7)

As Vizenor (1993) notes: "The colonists strained to tame the wild, the tribes and the environment. Now, high technologies overbear postcolonial promises and transvaluations; the tragic mode is in ruin" (p. 10). He points out the paradox in western culture that with so much emphasis on image, the visual, there is a corresponding demise of imagination. He cautions that too much surveillance and observation [research?] by academics abrogates narrativity—and orality. Trickster discourse is s-s-stuttering; it is pregnant pauses; it is the rhythm and beat of the unmanifest. It does not presuppose all silences to be the same. Hearing (and listening) surpasses seeing in trickster discourse. Trickster discourse is intentional gaps, ambiguity, equivocality, "narrative chance" arising in the silences of heard stories which are not voids needing fulfillment; it is discordance, "rumour and wild conversations" (Vizenor, 1993), making words flee from the middle creating ululations, semiomorphs—*glossolations*.

> The trickster narrative situates the participant audience, the listeners and readers, in agonistic imagination; there, in comic discourse, the trickster is being, nothingness and liberation; a loose seam in consciousness; that wild space over and between sounds, words, sentences and narratives. (p. 196)

Trickster discourse animates and liberates language. Trickster discourse creates contradiction between presence, absence, and silence, leaving no mechanistics for representation. It is not about prescription, but wonder, chance, and coincidence.

> Trickster narratives are suspensive, an ironic survivance; trickster metaphors are contradictions not presentations of culture. The peripatetic trickster is a deverbative narrative in translation, a noun derived from a verb, an elusive name that bears the shadows of the heard in active narratives and the tension of nominalism. (Vizenor, 1994, p. 170)

Trickster discourse provides labyrinthine language directed toward different knowings, refigurations of what is possible in the impossible. It is learning to transimbricate our own stories, to become epiphytes, bromeliads—airplants that need neither stem nor root, thriving from the nutrients of the air. They are botanical hitchhikers residing between tree and rhizome, seeking a place in the sun. Bromeliads are epiphytes, which host an array of small life but need no real host themselves. They just become.

Although "the trickster is real in those who imagine the narrative, in the narrative voice" (Vizenor, 1993, pp. 189–190), it is not the place of western intellectuals to simulate or appropriate the Trickster of First Peoples. That would be manifest manners. Besides, Trickster is not always something to celebrate, revere, or romanticize. Non-Aboriginal people might be unaware of the dangers of Trickster and might be better off seeking out tricksters in the histories and geographies of their own cultures, as well as the trickster within themselves.

Chance Operations, Poethics, and Silence

As 'we' in the western world shift and are being shifted from eco-environments to virtual environments, is it possible to have space for silence and stillness amidst the supersaturation of noise and visual stimuli? Is it possible to have silence and stillness in the dominant technology discourses so that other voices may be heard, so that students might hear their own voices and the voices of 'others'? For what reason should we listen? What are we afraid to hear?

The work of John Cage, poet and musician, presents rhizomatic potentialities with Deleuze's s-s-s-stuttering, in particular Cage's notions of "chance operations" and "poethics" as ways of living in the world. Chance operations offer ethical considerations and a politics of community radically different from how normalizing technology discourses are constructed and taught. N. Katherine Hayles (1994) suggests that chance operations are about probability and coincidence, the intersecting of independent causal chains, string theory. This is a place where irony and humour emerge from the conjunctions between independent worldlines. Hayles emphasizes the difference between a connection and conjunction, the latter unplanned and out of the narrator's control, aleatory encounters engaging *in* the world rather than *of* the world. Chance can outrun intention; it can find and break through the cracks in the foundations and standards and grids on the maps of shoulds and should nots. Chance operations are also about disrupting ordered notions of temporality; nonrelativistic time flowing only forward. Cagean temporality is asymmetrical and related to the notion of nonlinear fractal time—disordered time. It is about rhythm rather than harmony. The noncompressibility of chance, the randomness of simply letting words and sounds become, is another dimension of chance operations that works to disrupt standardization. It is what escapes, what surrounds, what exceeds, and what leaks out of the containers and structures of language, musical notation. What Cage offers is a form of anarchy, linguistic strategies that overwhelm intentionality without dismantling it, while at the same time encouraging individual responsibility. Chance operations are both intention and chance. Such delight in turbulence does not deny the messiness and ironies of real life.

Cagean poethics is the interrelationship between ethics and poetry, the ethical stances as we live in and through our language, art, and philosophy. Gerald Bruns (1994), looking at Cage's work, sees two predominant theories of ethics: one characterizing ethics in terms of our beliefs, desires, values, principles, perceptions, actions, and experiences; the other characterizing ethics in terms of how we respond to and respect others (not like me). In western culture, the leaning is toward the first theory, a morality based on perception by a perceiving moral agent with judgments based on having the right or wrong theory/cultural understanding/skin colour. For the second, claims of the other come before our reason and are often obstructed by our reason—*ratio mens causa sanitas* and so on down the line. The perceiving subject reaches, grasps, and reduces, removing alterity and strangeness. Bruns suggests that what is needed is to "turn the subject of perceptive intuition inside out" (p. 209), breaking up identity and cognition. Cage's second theory of ethics is about intimacy, intimate engagement within our wor(l)ds, not about consuming, possessing or exploiting. His second theory is not so much *about* the aboutness of knowing, but abiding *within/withas* reality—inhabiting it.

Poethics regard knowing as not only about knowing or not knowing, but *a willingness to not know* as the beginning of ethical action, thinking as letting go and receiving rather than capturing and assembling/ordering. Cage's poethics is about engaging in life, in the world in a way that "presupposes a condition of responsiveness, of openness and reception as against grasping and penetration" (p. 212). This mutual reading has significant implications for rethinking technology curricula, as well as for our questing for knowledge, a project that Gerald Bruns suggests is a pathos of the Descartesian/Kantian legacy where the isolated subject knows the world through purchase at the cost of its place. I hear echoes of Kroker and Weinstein's (1994) "will to virtuality," reclining and giving up of the body, mind, soul in the real and moving into cyberrealities; moving from our senses in physical weather to the virtual privileging of the Weather Network. Our methodological choices have been to ignore or try to contain and control weather/whether. Making meaning does not mean more knowledge or information. It can mean listening, leaving open space, being attentive and receptive.

Appreciating the music of John Cage requires a different relation to hearing/listening. Cage loved the whetherness of weather and held many of his concerts outdoors, "in the mi/d/st of whether—on the edge of rain" (Retallack, 1994, p. 244). He wanted to give himself and his performances over to chance, to the actual weather. His music speaks, beckons, apostrophes silence, invites randomness and contingency of sounds, including silences, of the worlds and words around and within us. Cage is not speaking of silence in the sense of an exclusion of the materiality of language, but a silence where there are always sounds if we allow ourselves to hear them. Othered voices. Cage's chance operations and poethics are ways of giving up control and letting sounds become. They s-s-scatter reasoned knowing, commute sentences, dissemble words, make room for recomposition and resonance, freeing the listener from controlling prescribed texts, freeing the I to become word-imps, nomadic-thinking nomadic subjects rather than simply techno-thinking techno subjects. Chance operations and poethics, like rhizomatics and trickster discourse, are being in the "centre of a leap" (Cage, 1961) rather than being at the top of the technological heap.

Rhizomatics, trickster discourse, narrative chance, chance operations, and poethics allow language to become diverse and spontaneous utterances contaminating the Eurocentric, capitalist structures of standardized technology discourses in education that flatten not only the terrain, but bodies. Instead of being trapped as passive bystanders in a value-system of materialism and rigid technical formulae, students, teachers, and community members become embodied, sexually and culturally differentiated, multiple, relational actors. Bodies flow and fluctuate, converse, cry, play, laugh in relationship not only with tools and computers, but with each other, as well as the land.

The sun is low. I gather up rhizomes, trickster discourse, narrative chance, chance operations, and poethics to guide me on this journey. It is time to set up camp and prepare to scale another plateau on the morrow. Good night, John. And, Coyote.

Hoooooooooooow!

Mesa Morphing Methodology

> Between the no longer and not yet lies the possibility
> of what was impossible under traditional regimes
> of truth in the social sciences.
> —Patti Lather, *Fertile Obsession*

> To mix and combine in the places in which you would
> analyze—isn't this hence a good methodology?
> —Michel Serres & Bruno Latour,
> *Conversations on Science, Culture, and Time*

I awaken to Coyote tracks on my tent, silhouetted against the sky. The scent of Coyote marking her/his terrain. Breakfast is a long way off. I leave my base camp to look for dry kindling and a splash of water. Today I must navigate through the dense, often impenetrable, methodological terrain as I search for a methodology of difference which, itself, does not become another form of coding and border making. The terrain is steep and rugged consisting of old growth forest, thick underbrush, green hanging life in every niche, overlaid with euroanalysis plants. That is just to get to my canoe. I pull on my hiking boots, apply sunscreen, and roll up my Gortex jacket in my day pack anticipating all sorts of weather/whether. I stuff my sunglasses into my fanny pack, and strap on a portable S.A.D. (seasonal affective disorder) light in case the journey becomes too overcast. I pause and wonder: Is there a possibility of curriculum inquiry that does not trample on the bodies and voices of 'others'? Is it possible to engage in research that is ethical, respectful, reciprocal, commensal, communal, joyful, rather than alienating? Keeping these questions at the foreground, I push my canoe from the shore and paddle toward this plateau-in-flux with trepidation and exhilaration. Once again on land, I follow different tendrils, roots/routes, in anticipation of mesa morphing a rhizo-methodology. I see coyote tracks in the soft moss, hear ravens circling overhead. *Wraakk. Raaa.* Maybe I will forgo breakfast today and attend to my relations.

Framing Methodology

I unfold some of the methodological maps I am familiar with so I have signposts for this journey into unfamiliar territory. Patti Lather (1991) writes about methodology as "the theory of knowledge and the interpretive framework that guides a particular research project" (p. 4). Theories and methodological frameworks of traditional western science are guided by the conventional notions of value-neutrality, impartiality, and rationality, which are supposed to produce unbiased, dispassionate, disembodied objectivity. Bingo. Welcome to Oz/Kansas/the Supreme Court/prison. As Donna Haraway (1991c) argues, these are stories that "signify a leap out of the marked body and into a conquering gaze from nowhere" (p. 188).

> The eyes have been used to signify a perverse capacity—honed to perfection in the history of science tied to militarism, capitalism, colonialism, and male supremacy—to distance the knowing subject from everybody and everything in the interests of unfettered power. (p. 188)

But of course that view of infinite vision is an optical illusion. Ann Game (1991) refers to this subject-object distancing of the gaze as a "sociological mirror," which is little more than a self-referential reflection of the researcher's understandings and experiences with the adjective *objective* being the hat rabbits are pulled from. Michel Foucault (1980) argues that such modes of objectification can be understood as practices of power/knowledge. Norms joined at the blip. These structures of scientific vision, with both external and internal modes of surveillance, turn everything into a resource for appropriation—females, the poor, Indigenous Peoples, this planet, and outer space—to move the western knowledge production project forward, with westerners being experts on everything and everybody, especially if they are another colour. It is the rainbow going backwards into the prism, emerging as white light—unrefracted, undiffracted.

With orthodox science in crisis, there is a proliferation of contending and overlapping paradigms, including positivist, interpretive, critical, and deconstructive sets of values (Lather, 1992). The sun breaks through. I unfold my flow diagram sketch of these paradigms and note their complexities, contradictions, and the impossibility of using such framings for universal curriculum inquiry. On a nearby cornice, an omniscient researcher is adamant about realist objectivist ontologies as s/he moves about as a spectator, a flâneur, using the seductive power of a disengaged and limitless vision to distance the subject from everybody and everything. "And like the god-trick, this eye fucks the world to make techno-monsters" (Haraway, 1991c, p. 189). For John Van Maanen (1988), four conventions are required for such a realist tale: absence of the author from the text; documentary form describing and redescribing "discovered" details into categories; translating routine events, slogans, and clichés of the "native" point of view; and interpretive omnipotence, pushing the data through proven grand theories. He suggests, "embarrassment with such realist conventions is one response in some fieldwork communities. When viewed as literary creations, realist tales may not seem so very real at all" (p. 67). When you get into a tight spot, they are not very useful in rappeling away from dangerous conclusions either.

A group of pensive-looking researchers is talking about ways to move about on an interpretivist map—hermeneutics, constructivism, symbolic interactionism, phenomenology, and naturalistic inquiry. The ontological positioning of this interpretivist map fluctuates between objectivism and subjectivism as meaning is sought in context. Working on the poles of this wet, torn map, one researcher acknowledges the possibility of multiple realities, ways of knowing, and stories, rather than accepting only universalizing narratives. Grand epics. Although the researchers working on this map question science's construction of women and Indigenous Peoples because they are "tied into developmental stage theories, the research adds to without problematizing the limits of such frameworks" (Lather, 1992, p. 94). They might be moving fast, but in what direction. Another shortcoming is that the research does not go beyond rationalist explanation.

Over the ridge, researchers examining a critical map want to know the world in order to work toward changing it. The different methods they use to negotiate change include participatory, neo-Marxist, praxis-oriented, Freirian, race-specific, minoritarian, and feminist, as well as permutations and perturbations of these methods. This map is marked up with hegemony theory, positing that the subjects need emancipation from the dominant ideologies of capitalism, patriarchy, and (neo)colonization. These researchers act as advocates or change agents. The *modus operandi* is the salvationist framework of resistance and transformation. Who is transforming whom? Into what? For whose benefit? Some of these researchers have learned to tread carefully so that they do not appropriate or romanticize the voices of the so-called oppressed, while claiming to see from their positions. Some have not been such good learners.

Orators spit and gesture, stand on big rocks, index fingers pointing to deconstructionist theories, working to disrupt and reshape the terrain, rather than simply resisting the dominant systems of knowledge production. As Jim Scheurich (1995) writes, "[r]esistance...is not freedom. Resistance is not an open possibility; it is a closed determination (p. 248). The borders of the deconstructionist's map are more blurred and fluid than most of the others—they like to leave space for more diverse and complex ways of telling data stories. This one claims there is *no fully knowable*, or *there there*. On one well-worn map, a researcher unthinks and rethinks her assumptions, beliefs, and values, working *with* the researched rather than *for, on,* or *instead of*. The *withness* needs lots of negotiation so that the researched/researcher positions become mutually reciprocal/beneficial, despite efforts to escape binaries. This tattered scotch-taped map is not an integration of positivist, interpretive, and critical maps, nor a paradigm shift from them; it co-exists with them as "post-paradigmatic diaspora" (Lather, 1992). Rather than single or totalizing narratives, their stories are "partial, locatable, and critical knowledges sustaining the possibility of webs of connections called solidarity in politics and shared conversations in epistemology...but not just any partial perspectives" (Haraway, 1991c, pp. 191–192).

Coyote and Raven have been sitting quietly in the shadows, listening to all this talk of framing methodology.

Mesa Morphing Methodology

Coyote pipes up, "Hey, what about pre-paradigmatic diaspora? Us pre-historics know all about that."

Raven, not to be outdone by Coyote, spreads her/his wings and says:

> a framework is not just an architect/ural
> or /tectonic manifestation of a blueprint
> for us it is the enactment of a respectful relationship
> with the rest of creation   which shares this earth   with us
> a framework is never a noun   it cannot be captured thus
> as a part of speech
> it is more than any words which attempt to denote it
> a framework   is a journey/ing   with . . . .
>
> frameworks yes we used what the newcomers called frameworks
> to gather our relations   the salmon nations
> these were our installations and properties and sets
> molding us to the places of the river which named us
> through our naming of them   the land languaged us
> with the breath it gave us   we spoke to identify   our connecting . . . .
>
> our frameworks and workings took into account the clarity (or not)
> of the water its speed its dervish its placidity its negotiativity
> we paid intimate attendance to geography   by the default position
> of being unseparated from it   rather than prepositionally related to it
> we were not speci/fically (as in species) different from salmon
> steelhead rainbow silver trout   oolichan   sturgeon dolly varden
> until we all started sprouting latin nomenclature . . . .
>
> our frameworks are not frames nor are they works
> they are the movement of forest and relations
> through mind   hand and spirit
> they shape our minds around themselves
> they bring it into organic functioning   retroactively
> fashioning themselves into us   through our co-operation. . . .
> (Cole, 2002, p. 452)

Who is doing the framing of whom? And through whose frames? Who is legitimate and who legitimates? Where are the foundries of authority? Who are its foundlings? What about those written off as being pre-historic by western academia although they have a history on this land for millennia? Who are the writers of history? Who are the speakers of pre-history? Is history itself not a Euro-construct? Raven continues:

> they write about 'working with' us except 'us' becomes 'them'
> first person plurality becomes third person (aka first person) singular
> in other words third person becomes first person
> first peoples have not even unbecome who we are
> alphabetically we mostly come after them in terms of authorship
> because we are both place of data collection as well
> as secondary or tertiary author/ities no matter
> what our surname begins with or theirs (Cole, 2002, p. 454)

Through the eyes of Indigenous Peoples, western research is yet another form of imperialism and colonization. For Linda Tuhiwai Smith (1999), western research "is probably one of the dirtiest words in the Indigenous world's vocabulary" (p. 1) because it has dehumanized Indigenous Peoples in the privileging of western epistemologies and methodologies. Smith suggests that research relating to Maori communities needs to engage *Kaupapa Maori* research, which is connected to Maori philosophy and cultural practices, and works to better the lives of Maori people. She cautions, however, that "there are powerful groups of researchers who resent Indigenous people asking questions about their research and whose research paradigms constantly permit them to exploit Indigenous peoples and their knowledges" (p. 17). As Russell Bishop (1998a) writes, the notion of "paradigms," and their shifting, is not from a Maori worldview. The academy abounds with academics who are 'Indian experts'—Aboriginal, Latin American, African, Asian, etc. experts. Ninety-five percent of books in Canada on First Nations are written by non-First Nations academics; 95% of research funding to study First Nations goes to non-First Nations academics. Sofia Villenas (2000) is concerned with western feminist grand narratives that "nam[e] for other women what constitutes oppression and emancipation" or "reverse the arrogance of Western-based feminisms" by defining Third World agency as resistance. "Certainly, resistance as interpretation may be a new wave of exoticism as it becomes chic and in vogue to frame people's actions as empowered 'resistance'" (p. 80). My partner, Peter, and I are concerned when we see First Nations graduate students being funneled into emancipatory or liberatory theories and methodologies, requiring them to take on the oppressor/oppressed binary, as well as salvationist theories. What about self-empowerment? This would mean a lot of uppity

'Indians' et al insisting that they are not minorities, especially when they make up the majority of the world.

> first nations people do not need to be empowered by others
> we can empower ourselves
> we are not deficient in knowings   needing filling of a Lacanian lack
> we have 15,000 years of knowings with this land
>
> we are narrators narratives voices interlocutors of our own knowings
> we can determine for ourselves what our educational needs are
>
> before the coming of the churches   residential schools   prisons
> before we knew   how   we knew   we knew
> (Cole & O'Riley, 2002, p. 148)

But, what would happen to the thousands of tenured non-Aboriginal 'Indian' experts in the academy? Perhaps they might think about studying their own culture to examine what it is in their culture that creates the desire to become "expert" on other.

Another form of framing research is coding and analyzing data. I am as concerned with coded/coding technology discourses as with finding ways to author(ize) my work without undue categorizing and incessant deciphering. One of the reasons for my unease about coding is that many students in technology education, in particular, are there because they are often coded as special needs students, categorized as low ability, low performing. Special needs is too often about gender and colour and socio-economics. Students are to undergo transformation and correction to have their wild knowledge mastered or (dis)solved. The current hot-wired solution is to plug technology education students into a shop-turning-into-computer-lab. Supposedly, students are to come out the other end of the electronic-lab-assembly-line education technologically literate—marketable commodities for sale to the highest bidder. Perhaps it is the teachers who have special needs, seeing their role as re-fabricating students into docile and obedient subjects, grist for the latest techno-mill. Educational technology is similar in its methods and methodologies; computers are used for games or drill and practice on special needs students, who too often are poor, speak languages other than English, or have coloured skin/perceptions. The special needs "gifted" students, on the other hand, are allowed room to explore hypermedia in ways that suit their particular learning styles. *All children are special and gifted*, though often these gifts are neither visible nor valued by those trained to seek out "mistakes" so that the students' deviant/deficient/different behaviour and ways of knowing can be re-formed (school) to fit within the dominant society's norms. Students are forced to colour within the lines of someone else's drawings and reality with White Out, and to follow those of the mainstream down their paths instead of creating their own.

Coding data discourses is not a distant relation of standardizing technology discourses—they are intimately related. Coding through white legitimation becomes a mobius, an ironic twist, though one taken with extreme seriousness—carved up and reduced to codes, then these codes are sustained until they are turned into large generalizations to explain and validate the universe and ourselves. However, the earth and people are *already valid*—as is. For some western researchers, this unanalyzed manifestation is not sufficient, so they set out to methodologically reify everything. They make up rational arguments to support data coding, because this is considered epistemologically more respectable than acausality or other kinds of nonrationalist methodologies. Tracking the perfect code. Head code. Finally, we (i.e. the West) convince ourselves that we have a better story, that we have gone *beyond*, that we have added to the western knowledge project—by reconstituting the already constituted. Our passion for the code is satisfied—for the moment.

Validity as Incitement to Discourse

Patti Lather (1993) writes of the possibility of validity as incitement to discourse and contributing to "an 'unjamming' effect in relation to the closed Truths of the past, thereby freeing up the present for new forms of thought and practice" (Bennett, as quoted in Lather, 1993, p. 676). Her desire is to "retain the term [validity] in order to both circulate and break with the signs that code it" (p. 674) as she opens the dialogue on her former notions of validity. Lather writes: "Offered as more problem than solution, my scandalous categories and the exemplars I have recruited as provocateurs of validity after poststructuralism are performances of a transgressive validity that work off spaces already in the making" (p. 683). *Ironic validity* acts much like Coyote taking on many forms and disguises, a shifting location of the knowable, foregrounding the insufficiencies of the one true story, displacing and decentring the universality and homogeneity of traditional technology discourses. It is a space of possibilities in the interstices of the dominating technology discourses and those in the wings, on/of the land. Ironic validity destabilizes practices of representation and "avoids simple reversal or simple replacement" (p. 677), repositioning and reshaping master narratives to allow more performative, dynamic discourses. *Paralogic validity* fosters differences; it undermines and implodes the controlling codes of standardized narratives, all the while acknowledging the existence of these codes. Recognizing the multiplicity of language games (including our own), paralogic validity "introduces dissensus into consensus, and legitimates via fostering heterogeneity" (p. 680). For example, the technology students and I disrupted the thematic codes of biotechnology, information technology, and control technologies that are articulated as capitalist production and electronic devices in their curriculum, by intersecting them with technologies of gender and race, reproductive technologies, environmental racism, sweatshop technologies, and so on. Biotechnologies, information technologies, and control technologies took on quite a different shape when looked at from these different standpoints. *Rhizomatic validity* "allows movement from hierarchies to networks...a journey among intersections, nodes, and regionalizations through a multi-centered complexity" (p. 680). It works within the ruptures of the pro- anti- western technology discourses as spaces to "let the contradictions remain in tension, to unsettle from within, to dissolve interpretations by marking them as temporary, partial, invested" (p. 681), including the researcher's own position(s). *Voluptuous validity* "posits the fruitfulness of situating scientific epistemology as shaped by a male imaginary. It asks what the inclusion of a female imaginary would effect where the female is other to the male's Other" (pp. 681–682). I also ask what the inclusion of Aboriginal epistemologies would effect where Aboriginal Peoples are other to the western other(ing)? And, what about knowings of/from the land?

For Gayatri Chakrovorty Spivak (1990), the word *valid* is a word "to dodge around the harsher and more legalistic *correct*," and she suggests instead more "scrupulous and plausible misreadings...without the cant of theoretical adequacy" (pp. 389–390). In a similar vein, Elizabeth Grosz (1995) rethinks the term *transgression* and writes of transgressing transgression by "questioning the presumptions of radicality—not from a position hostile to radicalism or transgression (as the majority of attacks are) but from within" (p. 4). To dissolve the "relentless forces of sameness" requires endless negotiation, "more inventive kinds of [inscription and] subversion" and "more joyous kinds of struggle we choose to be called into" (p. 6). James Scheurich (1996) cautions that postpositivist forms of validity are simply "masks that conceal a profound and disturbing sameness" (p. 49) because they are still part of the western knowledge project with both trustworthiness and validity as border making, bifurcating, and policing strategies; they fix norms, binarizing and demarcating what is valid and what is not. Scheurich (1996) writes:

> I fear the arrogance we enact "unknowingly." I fear my seeming lack of fear in proposing new imaginaries of validity, even transgressive ones. Perhaps, instead, we (I) ought to be stunned into silence—literally into silence, into a space of emptiness, into the clarity of the unknowing that appropriates no one or no thing to its sameness. (p. 58)

This resonates with John Cage's (1961) work on silence and the philosopher Stanley Cavell's conviction that "what we need is not more knowledge but the willingness to forgo knowing" (quoted in Bruns, 1994, p. 212) as a starting place for ethical action. The borders of successor forms of validity still remain an imperialist project; a process of denying what does not fit, or is outside of, the cultural understandings of western academic thought and subjectivities. "What is called for here, then, in the absence (fear) of silence, is a Bakhtinian dialogic carnival, a loud clamor of a polyphonic, open, tumultuous, subversive conversation on validity as the wild, uncontrollable play of difference" (Scheurich, 1996, p. 58).

Coming Out of the *Co*-Closet

As researchers, we bring our own knowings and experiences to our work. This particular journey is connected to my childhood and adolescence in the country swimming in and skating on the Skootamatta River, swinging on the fence gate, scaling the limestone cliffs, and climbing the huge pine, oak, and maple trees. Watching, listening. They come from taking risks in order to find life, and more than survival as a single parent, a friend, a partner, a worker, a trade unionist, a colleague, an academic; from sticking it out in technology education and finding ways to climb over/under/through/around the barriers and the prejudices placed in front of me. In retrospect, I have made many rhizomoves (although I had no such theories at the time). These street and backwoods smarts I learned as a child and adult, nurture and support me on my search for methodological and epistemological tools to enact a different methodology—*a methodology of difference*. They are not separate from the theories and methodologies I have learned in the academy, and they inform the attachments I make, and do not make, to particular academic discourses. For me, making meaning does not mean more knowledge or information or discovering the deep structures. It has to do with listening, leaving space, being attentive, receptive. Perhaps, methodology can offer a way to open ourselves to the *else/where* and *other /wise* of the world, to prepare for and participate with(in) weather/whether, blurring and humbling our vision and the politics of curriculum revisioning so that we can hear the silence/silents amidst the hyperstimulated noise and blinding illuminations and revisions of contemporary schooling.

  The co-participants and I plant our diverse knowings together rather than monocrop them. Because I am always already there in the languaging and mapping, as chief cartographer, I need to step aside and make every effort not to pull the co-participants into my own regimes of truth. The languaging and remapping needs to emanate from the historical and cultural experiences of the co-participants, as well as my own. How successful am I with not coding difference into the Same? What is hidden in my *co-closet* under the names of validity and ethics? As Scheurich (1996) suggests "it is in the particularities (the differences) of the local moment where the appropriate direction or choice may be conflict rather than collaboration, separation rather than unity, unknowing rather than knowing" (p. 57). Here, not knowing is a space of silence, which is not absence of sound, but a space of letting go of our desires including our desire to know other—knowing as not only about knowing or not knowing, but as letting go and receiving rather than capturing, assembling, and ordering.

On the plateau *Shapeshifting Tech Ed*, technology education students, a colleague from Kenya, and I work both inside and outside of the lines of Lather's transgressive validities, as we dance rhizomatically with Deleuze and Guattari, enacting Cage's chance operations and poethics, as well as Vizenor's narrative chance and trickster discourse. We look at the rhetorical nature of tech-talk, disrupting it as a regime of truth, displacing its historical inscription as industrial technology, and gesturing toward the problematics of representation of/for tech-talk in schools. Curriculum universals and standards are placed in question through examining the ruptures between the languaging of technology in schools and in the world. We consider the failure to represent—who and what is left out of the technology curriculum, and *what might be*, thereby displacing and remapping a different terrain, a terrain of difference. To counter(inter)rupt the Eurocentric male framings of biotechnology, information technology, and control technology, we examine their noninnocent implications on gender and race —reproductive technologies, environmental racism and sweatshop technologies in economically colonized countries. We work to decentre our own brand of common sense as we move among contestatory technology storylines, creating different connections. Rethinking institutional knowledge and practice, as well as our own assumptions about technology, is a place of humility, discomfort, and affirmation of different knowings, including students' knowings, which are often discounted as being of critical importance in education. We go AWOL, disrupt, and exceed the epistemological foundations of technology education by including the knowledges and experiences of those outside the Eurocentric male imaginary. I encourage a (re)consideration of technologies associated with females that have been ignored in curriculum revision(ing)s, as well as a discussion about how new technologies implicate and complicate women's lives, locally and globally. A colleague from Kenya talks with the students about some of the traditional technologies of her community, and about what western technologies and western development have done to her people, the Mkamba.

On the *A Dataplay* plateau a more joyful experiment to collect and write up the data for the educational technology segment of this journey is engaged. Taking as a point of departure from Scheurich's (1995) notions of "playing around" and experimentation with interviewing, as well as his new imaginary of "validity as the play of difference" (Scheurich, 1996), the educational technology graduate students and myself enact a *dataplay*, a performative analysis, a dress rehearsal including the dynamic (and appropriate) integration of technical cues into the action. The *dataplay* is an "excessive analysis" (Grosz, 1995), an experiment in holding together seemingly disparate elements—explosive rage, silence, tenderness, and humour. It is a mutually constituted co-production of creative language and imagination, an interaction of chance and selection intersecting with a specific time and place. Theorists from other plateaux resurface and insinuate themselves into the *dataplay* as characters, as does Coyote and pals. We seek isomorphic conjunctions by juxtapositioning or otherwise montaging dialogue, situation, and theory so that new connections and directions will syncretize from (and sometimes despite) the tech-talk paths. My voice is one voice in a chorus of many voices, and together we map a creative pastiche, a *rhizopoiesis*, a 'valid' piece of academic writing allowing for the whether of data stories that refuse and exceed containment, confinement, and codification. The writing, staging, editing, and rewriting act as both data and analysis without succumbing to interpretation.

    It is time to get back into my canoe and paddle to my campsite on the other side of the lake. I stop to filter water from the middle of the lake for tomorrow's journey. A log from the logged area on the north shore floats by. Curving shapes from my canoe and paddle dance with the reflection of the snow-capped mountains on the stillness of the water. I hear loons in the distance. Raven's *wraaak*. The haunting sounds of Coyote and her/his pals join in. I turn my canoe toward the shore.

Siting Tech Ed

> Modern morality consists in accepting the standard of one's age. For any man of culture to accept the standard of his age is a form of the grossest immorality.
> —Oscar Wilde, *The Picture of Dorian Gray*

> Will education be organized around the transmission of technical skills and specialized knowledge, as increasingly is the case? Or can education be focused on creating more cultivated human beings and the preconditions for a more democratic society? This would require a radical reconstruction of education.
> —Steven Best & Douglas Kellner, *The Postmodern Adventure*

> All my analyses are against the idea of universal necessities in human existence.
> —Michel Foucault, *Technologies of the Self*

Lucky thing I wore my hard hat to bed last night because it started raining tools and implements and tech-talk around dusk. It is handy to have a corrugated steel tent fly—hard to come by. Earplugs help, too. I knew today would be a tough day because of last night's weather. When I woke up, I looked around to see how my unprotected gear had fared. It was mostly demolished, but I knew it all inside out anyway, so it was just a matter of getting more supplies from the surrounding geography. There were tape measures, levels, hammers, screwdrivers, hand saws, tool belts, and welding rods scattered everywhere. It sounded like a male storm. I look up at the sky. No more surprises today, I figure, so I paddle down to the town on the next lake to check out *Deus Ex Machina* from the school board office library. On the same shelf I find *Homo Technologicus* and *Homo Cyberneticus* and decide to check them out too. I find a big easy chair and flip through a few of the pages. I notice that both texts are written by the same authors, and from the table of contents, they appear to have one and the same storyline—four by four. I decide to read a bit more before heading out.

The ~~Ford~~ Four Model Ts, or the Technification of Tech Ed

Once upon and through time, for at least a century, industrial education primarily taught boys such hands-on skills as woodworking, metalworking, mechanical repair, electricity/electronics, and drafting. Girls were taught domestic science, later called home economics or home ecology. Industrial education and home economics were generally offered as elective subjects, and by the late 1970s and 1980s enrollments were declining significantly as students were opting for university track courses. Industrial educators and craft teachers in Canada and many other industrialized countries realized that they were becoming extinct so there was a frenzy of activity to revise and update their curriculum stories, renaming them *Technology Education, Design and Technology, Technology Studies,* or *Technological Studies,* depending on the country, state, or province. In some places, technology education was constructed as a separate subject for study; in others as an emphasis to be included in all subject areas—technology-across-the-curriculum (e.g., Saskatchewan Education, 1988). In the United Kingdom and Wales, the *Design Technology Curriculum* (1989) incorporated several subject areas (craft, design and technology; home economics; art education; business education; and information technology) into one programme area. In North America, technology education curricula exist mainly as a reworking and rewording of industrial education/industrial arts. In 1981, a reconceptualized framework for industrial education, *Jackson's Mill Industrial Arts Curriculum Theory,* was developed in the United States. The authors came up with *four universal technical systems* they purported to be basic to every society—communication, construction, manufacturing, and transportation. These systems essentially mirrored the electronics/electricity, woodworking, metalworking, and automotive training in industrial arts. In 1990, the International Technology Education Association (ITEA), the Big Brother organization located in close proximity to the centre of political, military, and corporate power in the United States, did some reworking of these four categories and renamed them *content reservoirs*—biorelated, communication, production, and transportation. The four model Ts are maintained.

The distribution of these four model Ts for technology education, and its various per/mutations, has spread across Canada, and to many other countries in the industrialized world. In 1992, the British Columbia Ministry of Education joined the progress(ion) and reshaped their industrial education curriculum into *Technology Education: Primary Through Graduation Curriculum/Assessment Framework*, essentially mirroring the four categories as set out by the ITEA. They constructed four *content organizers* for the study of technology—information technology, materials and products technology, power and energy technology, and systems integration technology. In 1995, British Columbia did a semantic/semiotic play on these four categories, reassembling them into four *prescribed curriculum organizers*: communications, production, energy and power, and control.

Likewise, the New Zealand Ministry of Education (1995) retooled these four hegemonic categories for their *Technology in the New Zealand Curriculum*. They came up with production and process technology, materials technology, structures and mechanisms, as well as electronics and control technology. Two new categories, biotechnology and food technology, were added; however, these are limited to the design of products and production processes (O'Neill & Jolley, 1996/97). The Ontario Ministry of Education (2000) joined in with a similar grouping of four in *Technological Studies: Ontario Curriculum, Grades 11 and 12*—manufacturing technology, construction technology, communications technology, and transportation technology.

The technification of technology education can be further illustrated with the recent locating of technology education in British Columbia under the rubric of *Applied Skills*. As outlined in the British Columbia Ministry of Education (2002), *Prescribed Learning Outcomes:*

Communications
- At home and in the workplace, students will need to use technology in the processing and sharing of information, and communicate ideas using language, graphics, and technology.

Production
- Students build skills in designing and developing products and systems that improve the human condition.

Energy and Power
- Energy and power addresses the application of devices and processes that convert, transmit, and conserve forms of energy.

Control
- Control addresses the application of devices and processes used to manage, sort, control, and organize systems.

Let us take a look at what a student will learn about *Control technology* throughout their schooling to illustrate the instrumentalist, technicist orientation of current technology education curricula. Kindergarten and grade 1 students are to:

- identify common control devices in their homes and at school
- operate familiar control devices
- identify methods to control a device manually
- make a manual control device

Grade 8 students are to:

- design and construct a control device that senses, switches, or regulates
- compare ways that various control devices work, and explain their applications
- integrate electric, electronic, pneumatic, and mechanical control devices within a system
- demonstrate understanding of the concept of control by dismantling devices

The curriculum at all grade levels, and within any of the four Ts, is centred around problem solving, as well as product development and manufacture. Furthermore, there is a revocationalization of technology education with a revival of career preparation programmes through the reintroduction of *Automotive Technology, Carpentry and Joinery,* and *Drafting and Design* into the curriculum at grades 11 and 12.

Although significant amounts of funding have been expended to reshape the former industrial education curriculum into an area of study that would become a space "for all students," little has changed in the revised technology education curriculum. Technology education is still "shop," no matter what new labels are painted over the old categories. Sadly, the meaningful aspects of the former industrial education curricula—the artistic, spiritual, and craftspersonship—have been lost in the process as the curricula become reduced to mundane instrumentalism tied to neoliberalism and corporate capitalism. Technology education as currently designed is not about educating students to deal with the diversity and complexity of the technological world in which they live; rather it is about *training* students to become producers not only of products and technical systems, but also to become consumers. Shop 'til you drop.

Albert Borgmann (1984), an American philosopher, drawing primarily on the work of Martin Heidegger, refers to contemporary definitions of technology as the "device paradigm." He suggests a more comprehensive definition of technology, "the characteristic way we take up the world" (p. 35). Similarly, Ursula Franklin (1999), a Canadian physicist, writes about how contemporary articulations of technology are about power and control, downgrading personal experience and glorifying technical expertise. She describes technology as the sum total of what people do. Franklin writes that "there is a technology of prayer as well as a technology of ploughing; there are technologies to control fear as well as to control flood"(p. 8). Enacting more diverse and inclusive ways of communicating technology to students would better prepare them to recognize the range, complexities, and contradictions of *control technologies*, for example, so that they might see them as more than electronic paraphernalia, tools, and systems. This would also provide students with an opportunity to consider the *Control technologies* in/on their own lives, and to learn about the relationships between technologies, equity, social justice, and the environment.

Control(ling) Technology

Technology education in the United States has been defined by corporate and state interests through the Technology Education Act of 1986, with the ITEA becoming the principal promoter and machinery for the alignment of "economic supremacy with technological literacy" (Petrina, 2000b). The National Science Foundation and the National Aeronautics and Space Administration in the United States have given substantial financial support to the ITEA (1996) for *Technology for All Americans*, a project to standardize the study of technology in education. More recently, the ITEA (2000) has devised the document, *Standards for Technological Literacy: Content for the Study of Technology*, laying out twenty *standards* that focus on the *knowledge, skills, and attitudes* students are to acquire to enhance and intensify American global corporate capitalism. In Canada, many provincial technology teacher education associations have become ready, willing, and unquestioning conscripts of the ITEA, ensuring a northern migration of universals and standards into provincial technology education curriculum documents. *Technology for All Americans* is becoming *Technology for All Canadians*—*McTechnology*—fast-food technology serving thirty million in Canada alone.

The shift to standardize the conversation takes the con out of conversation, leaving a series of parallel monologues. Not only is the content for the study of technology technicized and standardized into "disciplinary technologies" (Foucault, 1979), but pedagogy has been reduced to the *design process* or *problem solving*, and assessment or evaluation has been abbreviated to *prescribed learning outcomes* ensuring that all students colour within the state and corporate-drawn lines. Félix Guattari (1995) writes:

> Everywhere the totalitarian machine is in search of proper structures, which is to say, structures capable of adapting desire to the profit economy. We must abandon, once and for all, the quick and easy formula: "Fascism will never make it again." Fascism has already "made it," and it continues to "make it." (p. 244)

Technological literacy defined as problem solving has been making its way into technology curriculum content and teacher education programmes in North America, whereas *technological capability* and/or design in the United Kingdom, New Zealand, and Australia are the preferred terms. Problem solving and/or design are the most deeply entrenched practices of technology education (Petrina, 2000a). The purposes of problem solving and/or design vary little from one curriculum document to another, and centre on the notion of finding technological solutions to human needs and wants. Although not excluding nontechnological solutions, problem solving or design is effectively promoted as *the one way* to teach technology education, and within the framework of problem solving, only one approach is identified, the technological method, which has its roots in the scientific method.

Stephen Petrina (1993) contends that problem solving is "a heuristic whose efficacy is limited to systems thinking. Methodological claims to the 'technological method' are bereft of any epistemological grounding within the history, philosophy, or sociology of technology" (p. 72). The concept of knowledge that is mobilized is instrumental in the extreme and is concerned with control, privileging analytical and hierarchical thinking over holistic thinking while downplaying intuitive, emotional, aesthetic, and spiritual dimensions of human experience. What if students end up with different and unexpected results that might be as good as, or even better than, what they had started out to do because they worked from a different worldview and/or used other than problem solving or design techniques? Would this be considered a mistake? Would the students be considered technologically illiterate?

Ivan Snook (1996) writes of the banality of the design and making emphasis of technology discourses and suggests a more critical technological literacy in schools:

> Technical problems are not the only problems of life and arguably are not the main ones: we face ethical problems, relationship problems, financial problems, emotional problems and, of course, political, social and cultural problems. The school should help its students with all these sorts of problems. It is a blatant ideological take-over to imply that the only real problems are those related to altering the material world and making money. (p. 10)

Snook looks at a project to create a fashionable garment. For there to be critical technological literacy as part of this project, the fashion industry itself would require serious questioning before embarking on any design-and-making project. Students might be asked to consider the role of fashion artificially generated for profit? the grounds for stiletto heels? bras and bikinis for nine year olds? tight jeans for adolescents? Students might take field trips to garment factories, cottage industries, cotton fields, the homes of knitting women, and the backstages of the modeling industry. They might talk to the workers, mostly female and recent immigrants, about their wages, hours of work, and working conditions. This would be threatening to powerful business interests (i.e., the garment trade, a big part of the fashion industry).

The desiccated technical rationality of problem solving reflects methods that have been practiced in such male-dominated areas as science, the military, engineering, and industry for centuries. Problem solving sets up the world as a series of problems that lend themselves to technical solutions, encouraging the phantasm of control and technofixes. Technonarcissism. Within technicist framings, technology is assumed to be good and a means to extend human potential for *all*. There is little or no space for discussion about who the *all* is, or technology's potential to create human and environmental problems and disasters. For Donna Haraway (1991c), questing for universals and standards is nothing less than reductionism "when one language...must be enforced as the standard for all translations and conversions" (p. 187). The desire to configure standards resonates with what Sandra Harding (1986) refers to as the longing for the "one true story" that has been the psychic motor for western science. The "real world of technology" (Franklin, 1999) has been crafted into supposedly stabilized, homogeneous categories, which have become the codes, the facts, and the artefacts prescribed for the study of technology. These rudimentary machinations to limit the study of technology into neatly packaged so-called universals claimed as accurate or valid representations, vastly underestimate the ambiguity, complexity, and indeterminacy of technology, of the students, and of the world. Universalism, standardization, and prescription in education are simply new masks on the old prejudices and exclusivities, ensuring that heterogeneity, questioning, and resistance disappear. For industrial educators, or anyone for that matter, to think that they can capture or represent technology in these ordered taxonomies is an indication of the modernist desire to direct and encapsulate reality. As Russell Bishop (1998b), a Maori scholar, writes:

> When one curriculum, one set of knowledges and narratives is constructed as representing 'the truth' or 'the real,' and it obliterates or marginalises alternative conceptions, it is an act of violence. (p. 8)

The prescribed abstract masculinities and noninnocent cultural narratives for technology education are decontextualized, reductive monads of meaning that inscribe tightly bound generalized categories to predict, control, and *re*-form industrial education into technology education through "the privilege of partial perspective" (Haraway, 1991c) of a relatively small and parochial cultural community. Mark Sanders (1995), writing specifically about the *Technology for All Americans* project, suggests that technology educators "should welcome those different models while unabashedly promoting those which have made us so successful for the past century" (p. 3). The "us" is male and white and inclined to technical and trades interests. The revisioned curricula centre on industrial design, reflecting the former industrial educators' own backgrounds and interests, which are within the browse and tether of western science, engineering, and industrial technologies, and their accompanying ideologies of growth, efficiency, productivity, competition, and consumption. Technology discourses give the impression of "sovereign judgement, of stable subjectivity legislated by 'good' sense, of rocklike identity, 'universal' truth, and justice" (Massumi, 1987, p. ix). The movement to tighten technology discourses into standardized components creates an enclosed and impermeable border, controlling and sealing off interactions between the sanctioned discourses and the time, space, and bodies of other technology storytellers. Unfortunately, industrial educators appear to be unable to see that the knowledges and methods that have served them so well for decades refer only to their own realities. This is *not to say that their realities are false or invalid,* rather that there are other realities. Based on my own experience, as well as the experiences of other females (see Braundy, O'Riley, & Petrina, 2000), when any of these other realities are voiced they are seen as threatening the status quo. "Silencing...is less a matter of preventing speech than of having already assigned it to the categories of obsolescence, as then literally unnecessary to be *heard* in the condition of the present" (Watkins, 1993, p. 99).

Realities beyond the understandings of those who have dominated the (re)visionings of technology education will remain opaque. There is too much to lose from xeno-clarity—the clear vision of strangers—and from having different and at times contradictory ideas accepted. What might be clear—fuzzy thinking/

rational/common sense/obvious—to one person might be anything but to another. Industrial educators have imposed their own preconceptions through naming and categorizing the unknowable, believing that having done this, the contingency, indeterminacy, and complexity of technology can now be located, constructed, and knowable as framed into what Guattari (1995) refers to as "micro-crystallizations....They would like to make us believe that we can do nothing but stand with our hands tied in the face of the hysterical gesticulations and paranoiac manipulations of local tyrants and bureaucrats of every kind" (p. 239).

Another attempt to standardize technology education is the move from *Homo faber* to *Homo cyberneticus*. For a decade, many industrial education shops have been undergoing renovations, refitting with prepackaged technology labs, primarily from the United States, such as *Lab 2000*, which was costing in at approximately $250,000 per classroom. These labs consist of a series of computer and multimedia stations to teach the standardized domains of knowledge in an anaesthetized and controlled virtual context. School districts with smaller budgets have renovated industrial education shops and (re)wired them computerizing-mechanics, woodworking, metalworking, electronics, and drafting. Computer numerical controlled lathes, computerized diagnostic equipment, robotics, and computer drafting programmes such as AutoCAD are now commonplace. The industrial green walls and hardware are being repainted in pastels or brighter colours. Scattered around the labs hang pictures of girls and students of colour smiling into computers; these pictures are often advertisements for that particular computer lab company. Live plants are cropping up everywhere. Instead of the dark blue or green shop coats worn as industrial educators, technology teachers wear white lab coats or street clothes.

These technology labs have been designed primarily by ranks of technological "experts"—engineers, scientists, systems analysts, computer programmers, manufacturers, and so on, who have (in)vested interests in marketing their ideologies, as well as their hard- and softwares. Annual conferences of the ITEA, for example, are in major part, huge computer lab trade shows. Applied Educational Systems, Lego Dacta, Lab 2000, Principles of Technology, CADKEY, Pitsco, Paxton Action Labs, MTL Mobile Factory 2000, AutoCAD, and so on, use these conferences to sell their predesigned learning systems to technology educators. Very often the first lab is offered at prices teachers and school administrators have a hard time refusing. With the opting for prepackaged learning, technology educators relinquish their particular local knowings, as well as their autonomy as teachers in the classroom. They are becoming managers of curricula designed by those who have a narrow and self-interested understanding of technology, and little or no understanding of education. Education has become a commodity, a subcategory of the stock and bond market. For Deleuze (1995), "the quest for 'universals' of communication should make us shudder" because they are "permeated by money" (p. 175); "marketing is now the instrument for social control and produces the arrogant breed who are our masters" (p. 181).

Tech Ed as Capital Ad/venture

Deleuze (1995) cautions that the disciplinary societies Michel Foucault wrote about are "stealthily" being turned into "control societies" in which schools and other publicly funded institutions, such as hospitals, crown corporations, and prisons, have given way to business, and to "frightful continual training, to continual monitoring of worker-schoolkids or bureaucrat-students" (p. 175). The chant of 'lifelong learning' has infiltrated education, a neo-Fordist call for perpetual training as a response to perpetual changes in the marketplace. Technology discourses in education are very much intertwined with IWC (integrated world capitalism) and/or ME (market economy). High tech capital needs differentiated by gender, culture, and socioeconomics are prioritized, necessitating education for mass ignorance, docility, and malleability. The rights of business come before the rights of children, liberal education, social justice, and environmental responsibility.

Snook (1996) asks if technology education is a new subject or a new ideological strategy? He sees technology education as a patsy for businesses to get their feet firmly grounded in education and questions the epistemological warrant for technology as a separate subject area. "Technology curriculum...is neither vocational in any interesting sense; nor is it liberal. It is a domesticating curriculum aimed at producing passive followers of other people's agendas" (p. 10). Snook believes that technology education is about creating a new species of child—the kind technology and business want them to become. Corporate interests are calling for a reliable reserve of adaptable, flexible, loyal, expendable, trainable workers for the twenty-first century—human capital (Harvey, 1989; Noble, 1993). Technology educators appear to be unequivocal in their response to the call. Why is there so little resistance to students becoming conscripts (Taylor & Johnsen, 1993)—electronic soldiers for the New World Order, Inc.? The language in technology education curricula reverberates with phrases related to jobs and corporate capitalism: preparing students for the workplace, preparing students to work effectively in a changing technological society, creating workers for the future, exploring and pursuing technological careers, enhancing global competitiveness, and maintaining and sustaining economic progress). Here is a telling comment from John Sculley, Apple CEO and Chair of the National Center on Education and Economy in the USA:

> We in the personal computer industry are really in the behaviour-changing industry. We have the challenge to create the tools that fundamentally are going to change the way people learn, the way they think, the way they communicate, the way they work. (Noble, 1993, p. 12)

Higher-order thinking (aka problem solving and design) often teams up with the progressive social constructivist conversation, which presumes that students are architects of their own learning.

Although students are making *cyber*connections and constructing electronic fantasy worlds, they are having less time for more substantive struggle for meaning, character, and engagement in the material world. "You would suppose that interactive learning would have something to do with people talking and meeting, sharing ideas maybe face to face....It turns out, however, that all that's required to earn the label of 'interactive' these days is to involve a computer somewhere" (Winner, 1996, p. 4). Jacques Ellul (1990) is also concerned about the lack of critical dialogue regarding computerized learning for children. He is particularly concerned about enticing children to use computers through the use of games, a practice he refers to as "terrorism in a velvet glove."

Suzanne Damarin (1993) raises questions about what teachers are really teaching students as the emphasis in schools moves to visual learning and students learn to become "gazers" and "perceivers." She encourages educators to think about whether they are teaching students to become "tourists or travellers"?

> Playful world travelling, the comfortable movement from one knowledge situation to another, requires that "arrogant perception" be absent from the travelling learner/knower and from the situated knowledge community. Here "perception" refers to the knowledge/attitude with which a person meets a situation. A person's perception (of another situation) is arrogant when it exists or is expressed in subtle or overt ways which devalue the other or the situation. When an arrogant perceiver is around, the cooperative construction of knowledge from a shared standpoint or situation is impossible. (p. 28)

Damarin asks how a perceiver can be in the same "critical plane as the objects of knowledge" in virtual learning situations. Communicating via computer from the situated position of white privilege to a First Nations child on a First Nations reserve, or to other Indigenous Peoples, is not the same as "living in the village" (Cole, 2000a). Damarin writes that such learning does not create "situatedness," and she urges educators to consider seriously how "to educate for and honor the travel, not only to virtual worlds, but also back from them" (p. 31).

Whereas the electronic global reach is indeed far and broad, students' perceptions of their own bodies and the physical environment, as well as the interrelationships between these are abbreviated. Bodies collapse into a virtual spatiality of screen/surface (Grosz, 1992; O'Riley, 1994). The mind is given precedence over body, practice, and spirituality. It is difficult to feel and fight issues as a distant observer when sitting in front of a television or computer screen, reclined and virtually engaged. Feeling and resisting require bodies, and a lot of hard work. It is not a surprise that today's students are so out of shape, out of touch. Regardless, education appears to be running as fast as it can to be caught up in the Net—wired classrooms, wired curricula, wired teachers, wired students. Now wireless.

Standardizing how students are to learn and how teachers are to teach is a very serious political act. As Haraway (1991c) suggests, "this world-as-code is, just for starters, a high-tech military field, a kind of automated academic battlefield, where blips of light called players disintegrated...each other in order to stay in the knowledge and power game" (p. 185). Is technology called *high* tech because it is that of western societies? What makes western technology higher? Than what? Than whose? Is virtual learning yet another form of colonization, the next frontier? Colonizing and domesticating technology discourses by organizing so-called systems of knowledge organizes and controls people. The constricted codings of technology education obscure and dismiss the epistemologies, ontologies, and technologies of the majority of the world. The "possibility of the radically heterogeneous" (Spivak, 1976) is reduced and reformed to fit the resurrected Enlightenment humanist project of technology education, which is inescapably implicated in the flows of neocolonialism, corporate capitalism, and other contemporary declensions of mercantile and totalitarianism hubris.

In *Learning to Divide the World: Education at Empire's End*, John Willinsky (1998) suggests that the "legacy of imperialism" in education is its continued "desire to unconsciously instill standards and values in the young" (p. 96). "Imperialism has been transformed in recent years into a new form of global economy no longer dominated by a handful of European powers" (p. 53). Global competition has become much more than a nation striving for economic viability as it links up to new forms of imperialism, technology, and capitalism.

> We propose the term *technocapitalism* to signal the new synthesis and modes of capital, science, and technology....characterized by a decline of the state and enlarged power for the market, accompanied by the growing strength of transnational corporations and governmental bodies and the decreased power of the nation-state and its institutions. (Best & Kellner, 2001, p. 11)

With the ongoing FTAA (Free Trade Area of the Americas) negotiations, there is reason for concern about the increasing corporate intrusion into education, and about students becoming disciplined and marketable commodities, human capital, technological components for the global factory.

Universalization and standardization are neo-imperialist impulses that work to divide, particularize, and fragment students, while simultaneously creating their desire to become incepts in the New World Order, Inc. In its present form, technology education appears to be a campaign of (re)producing *techno*-codependents, *techno*-progeny. It is concerned with "educating taste," a desire not only for consumer products which are most often beyond the possibility of most people, but also functions to extend, authorize, legitimize, and proliferate sociocultural class relations (Watkins, 1993). Technology education has become an apparatus to create "desiring-machines" (Guattari, 1995), which are not the gadgets and contraptions but the conversion of production into the mechanism of individual consumption. Unlike a tool, which is an agent of contact, the machine is recurrent—repetition *without* difference. "Desiring-machines are not in our heads, in our imagination, they are *inside the social and technical machines themselves*" (p. 137), inside the current technological regime which decides on its size and ends. Here the relationship is that of peopling the social technical machines, being ourselves one of the parts. Guattari stresses that this is "not a matter of ideology, but a machination that brings into play an entire group unconscious characterizing a historical epoch, the tie between these attitudes and the social and political field is complex, although it is so indeterminate" (p. 148).

According to William Taylor and Jane Johnsen (1993), standardized testing was introduced in schools in the USA during the war years, institutionalizing the sorting of humans for their usefulness as technological components, human resources for commerce and the military. The *Technology for All Americans* project perpetuates these historical practices of linking education with corporate and military interests. Taylor and Johnsen note that since the post-Sputnik paranoia with its "nation at risk" and "crisis" fallout, technological experts have been called in to *save* schools. In the case of technology education, intervention and control of education by powerful state industrial-military state apparatuses is evidenced with the funding from the NSF (National Science Foundation) and NASA (National Aeronautical and Space Association) to apply a military systems approach in support of creating discipline-centred standardized curriculum, engineered for classroom applications.

In *The Classroom Arsenal: Military Research, Information Technology and Public Education,* David Noble (1991) writes of the influence on corporate leaders by contentious studies predicting a shortage of skilled workers, and a need for high tech skills, and in turn their considerable influence on education. In *The Regime of Technology in Education,* Noble (1993) comments on the irony of corporate insistence on schools producing human capital for high tech corporations, while these very corporations "are busy lopping off millions of present and future high skill jobs in the name of productivity and competition (while also tapping cheaper skilled labour overseas)" (p. 7). "Capitalist relations of production are not simply established on the scale of great social groupings; from the cradle onward, they shape a certain type of producer-consumer individual" (Guattari, 1995, pp. 249–250). There is little debate about what students and community might be losing out in their education by being funnelled into the workplace so early in their lives, or what may happen when the company pulls out, and the students are left with limited skills and no jobs. Evans Watkins (1993) refers to the creation of a societal order that binds particular classes, races, and genders within society to a particular work culture as "class-as-lifestyle." Career preparation programmes play a role in this by keeping students "frozen in adolescence," and "condemned to the terminal obsolescence of throwaways" (p. 216). Many of the boys in my study had their social positioning already imprinted into their psyche, referring to themselves as "the dummy kids in the dummy wing, with the dummy teachers," expendable labour for the burgeoning service economy so important to consumer culture.

For Noble (1993), it is no coincidence that the retooling and restructuring of schools is taking place at the same time that military-corporate interests are retooling and restructuring. "Restructured schools have less to do with improvements in education than with the easy assimilation of technology into curriculum" (p. 10). Education is a crucial market for self-interested corporate marketeers conjoined by technocrat politicians and "a legacy of military fantasy" (p. 12), a powerful regime alien to education and desperate for new markets. Much of the research and development of these companies has been lavishly bankrolled by the Department of Defense in the United States. Noble writes that the "military spends seven dollars for every civilian dollar spent on educational technology research. Each year the military spend as much on educational technology research as the Department of Education has spent in a quarter of a century" (p. 7). Noble gives examples of many prominent educators touting the military and industrial language and practices of problem solving skills, learning strategies, integrated learning systems, and authentic performance assessment, who have received military/corporate funding: John Seeley Brown of Xerox and its Institute of Research on Learning; Seymour Paper of the MIT Artificial Intelligence Lab and Media Lab, and developer of LOGO (originally funded by the Office of Naval Research); Robert Gagne and Robert Glaser of the National Academy of Education; Lauren Resnick, Director of the Learning Research and Development Center, University of Pittsburgh. Noble cautions educators to pay attention to the number of CEOs who are underwriting curricula for schools and reinventing education in their own image. Corporate America is a huge patron pushing computer technologies in education. Apple's *Classrooms of Tomorrow* and similar corporate high tech excursions into the classroom are billing themselves as research and development, as distinct from sales or marketing ventures. Langdon Winner (1996) refers to the current entrepreneuring of education through corporate and school joint ventures as "technoglobalism's assault on education."

Contemporary capitalist production and exchange are at an excessive state of accelerated "time-space compression" (Harvey, 1989) reconceptualized as a process of "hyperaccumulation" (Schoonmaker, 1994). Virtually instantaneous transborder data flows allow corporations to control geographically dispersed service and commodity production under the flexible accumulation regime. Computer and multimedia technologies play a major role in advanced capitalism and the ensuing political, sociocultural, and environmental struggles (Robins & Webster, 1999). With the ascendancy of economic globalization, there has been increased economic disparity, with the richest 20% of the world's population increasing their share of the world income from 70% to 85% over the last 30 years.

Curriculum revisionists, for the most part, appear to have taken on the role of corporate propagandists, spreading the gospel of business and preaching survival of the fittest. *He* who has the most, and most powerful, technologies wins. Or will he? Bill Joy (2001), cofounder and Chief Scientist of Sun Microsystems, former co-chair of the presidential commission on the future of IT research, and co-author of The Java Language Specification, writing in *Wired* magazine, gives a very clear warning about the very real and imminent dangers of technology ending up in the hands of an increasingly tiny elite who will have control over the masses, as well as the ability of technology to rapidly outsmart humans.

> It is most of all the power of destructive self-replication in genetics, nanotechnology, and robotics (GNR) that should give us pause....We have had in hand for years clear warning of the dangers inherent in widespread knowledge of GNR technologies—of the possibility of knowledge alone enabling mass destruction. But these warnings haven't been widely publicized; the public discussions have been clearly inadequate. There is no profit in publishing dangers. (p. 248)

With the current worries of nuclear weapons and biological weapons at home and elsewhere, such as *E. coli*, anthrax, and smallpox, technological literacy takes on a whole new urgency. How were these technologies allowed to proceed in the first place? Where is there place for public dialogue? When and how will this male decapitation of public debate end?

According to Best and Kellner (2001), our current "technoculture" has four features. The first is the technification of the world so that everything we (westerners) do is permeated, and mediated, by technologies in the form of "new gadgets and machines" and a "sea of commodities." Western technologies have also expended the lives and the geographies of nonwestern peoples. The second feature is an overdependence on technology, because more and more of what we do is being taken over by western 'high' tech. Rather than liberating people from manual labour, the new technologies intensify production, as well as create unemployment. "Third, a technoculture is distinguished by the hegemony of techno-consciousness....Information replaces knowledge" (p. 216), and fourth, the substitution of "commercially and technologically mediated communities" are replacing social life—shopping malls, email, distance education. Life online. As Neil Postman writes, "technopoly consists in the deification of technology, which means that the culture seeks its authorization in technology, finds its satisfaction in technology, and takes its orders from technology (1993, pp. 63–71). Technology discourses in education exemplify both technoculture and technopoly. Standards have been created; order out of disorder, chaos, and freedom. It is vital that technology education be opened to difference(s) leading to the "liquidity of the pretended universality" that "secures against political and social contingencies" (Guattari, 1995, p. 226).

More than paradigm shifts or ideological shifts will be needed to break with the hegemony of technology education curricula that privilege some and overlook most others, and disregard the environment. To create equitable, culturally respectful, socially just, and environmentally responsible curricula will require remapping the focus from the individual to community and from progress to sustainability, as well as enacting western and non-western epistemologies and technologies as *equivalent conversations*.

Back at my campsite, I boil some water for tea. I watch the fire as it dances against the silhouetted trees and wonder what I can do to make a difference in a curriculum area that seems slammed shut to difference(s). I get out the fountain pen my daughter, Lee, bought me when I was teaching in Aotearoa/New Zealand, lean back against my backpack and begin writing.

gridding   tightening   framing
gasping for breath   suffocating
how can there be life in this place?
how can there be love?
without either of these
how is it possible to live in story and spirit?
within these shop walls and computer labs

I cannot pry open the grids held in place
with words   standards   machines
their truths   their words of certainty
my mind   body   and soul whisperings   so uncertain

and yet I know that life can be made in these places
when eyes and hearts   doors and windows   are opened
when I unlace my boots   and let my feet touch the earth
where spirit and body have a place to dance

Shapeshifting Tech Ed

> When girls start school, the discourse they learn is
> that of he/they (il(s)), or the between-men culture
> (l'entre-il(s)).
> —Luce Irigaray, *Je, Tu, Nous*

> Hey, wait a minute! I have technologies too.
> —Coyote, *personal communication*

The ground is trembling, the birds are not singing, the four leggéds are gone. I hear the whining and clunking of gears and shafts and power take-offs, the whirring of saws, feel the falling of trees, the rumbling of logging trucks as they make their way through the switchbacks to the sawmill two valleys over. How has it all happened so fast? They are already putting up hundreds of dams for power and are putting through pipelines. I am thirsty, but the stream has dried up. There are just rain puddles that animals will not drink from. Murmurs of those drowned out in the noise and stimulation of progress narratives can barely be heard. Shhh! Listen. The voices of women and girls, the unborn, speaking about the gendering of technology, the technologizing of women's bodies, sweatshop technologies, biotechnologies, and reproductive technologies. If I listen closely I can also hear voices of the homeless people on the streets of Vancouver, displaced peoples, refugees of economic globalization, the landless, farm workers, seasonal workers, the differently abled, otherly inclined. Aboriginal and Indigenous peoples are wondering how to counter the effects of colonial education and western technologies on their communities and their land. Hold out? Sell out? Buy in? What's the difference? Better to sell than have it taken for national security or the greater good. Who is there to problematize the racialized distinctions between high and low tech? It is a distinction easily minted: Everything white is high. Everything else is low or no. However, who is in conversation with (respect to) the environment? Who is concerned with the abdication of environmental responsibility in technology discourses? Right—dotdaddy@fastbucks.me. Progress has arrived. Development. Already the plans are being implemented for uranium mines, aluminum smelters, hydro dams, nuclear power stations, chemical plants, oil wells, fractionating towers, garbage and toxic waste dumps, tens of thou-sands of miles of asphalt and concrete, all necessary, all vital for global technocapitalism. Are these not anti-environmentalisms? How has it come to be that gender, culture, and the environment do not share an equitable space in the pro/com/motion of design and production narratives for technology education? Does consideration of corporate global technocapitalist responsibility for environmental/human impacts put a kibosh/governor on profit/ability?

The storm has passed, but there are a few dark clouds in the sky. Regardless, I have decided to paddle over to the next plateau where I am to meet up with the technology education grade 11 and 12 students I have been working with for several months. There is one female student in the class. Dr. mutindi ndunda has agreed to meet up with us today, and I suspect that Coyote may make an appearance. Expecting all kinds of weather/whether, I put on my Gortex jacket and pants, stuff my tape recorder and notebook into a small drysack, grab a power bar and my nalgene bottle filled with the water I filtered last night, and push off from shore. A female moose and her calf move back from the shore as I pass by, and two eagles circle overhead.

Remembering Tech Ed's Gendered and Industrial Roots

John Willinsky (1998) writes that difference is the intellectual engine of the empire and suggests educators consider "how the lessons that were drawn from centuries of European expansion continue to influence the way we see the world retain their position in education" (p. 25). No curriculum area is exempt. Even so, technology discourses are especially implicated/imbroglioed in the persistence and continuance of the gendered relations and colonial rule of classifying and categorizing knowledge as an "apparatus of imperialism...to enumerate, order and identify a world of difference" (p. 27). Willinsky argues emphatically that "remembering" how the legacy of imperialism has created difference in education is an important and urgent survival strategy for extricating ourselves from the productivist mode. This writing journey is a remembering of the legacy of imperialism in technology education, including its historical divisions of masculine/feminine, us/them, and culture/nature. It is also a resurfacing, realizing, and regeneration of what has been dismissed or otherwise obliterated. It is an effort to remap different discourses and to enact and inscribe a "critical geography" of the "historical divisions out of which we have fashioned ourselves as educated people, even as we work together to move beyond our current understanding of an inexorably divided world" (Morrison, 1992, p. 20).

One manifestation of imperialism is how the history of technology is taught. If it is taught at all, it is basically a short history predominantly chronicling the triumphs and benefits of western technology (Needham, 1993; Petrina, 1993; O'Riley, 1996). The students I worked with have little historical understanding of technology. Technology for them was about now and in the future, mirroring how technology is denoted in their curriculum, in spite of the fact that they live on land that has at least fifteen thousand years of human technological history.

> James: Technology is the way of the future.
> Fabio: Technology is new stuff. A refrigerator has been around for a long time.
> Derek: We should think about the next frontier, which is space. We would be more driven to getting off earth. As there is more stuff to do off earth that will support us. If we start heading for the moon and stuff, that will open up a whole new area.

A principal stated goal in the revisions is to produce producers and consumers for the global economy, with claims that this is the way of the future—intimating an improvement on the present. The past is passé; our future is in the future. "Forgetting" problems created by technology has been essential for the cultural explosion of the West. As Best and Kellner (2001) write:

> Capitalist "creative destruction" does not merely entail the "destruction" of past successes in the drive to continually construct something new, but also involves the destruction of firms, competitors, communities, traditional cultures, workers' lives and families, wildlife, and the envi-

ronment in the constant lust to accumulate profit and revolutionize production. (p. 136)

Limitless perspectives and conquering discourses of continued discovery, in/out/re/sourcing other, and marketing the novel are not called into question, rather they are the *modus operandi* of technology education. Do unto—before somebody else does.

A major dimension of the legacy of imperialism influencing contemporary technology education discourses is its history as industrial education, which for over a century was based on the sexual division of labour. Girls were taught lessons in domesticity, especially childrearing and cooking, and boys learned how to use tools to ready them for the labour market. Foods and textiles have been added to many technology education curricula without questioning the gendered foundations of technology education, consequently creating the de/il/lusion of *value-neutral* or *girl-friendly* curricula. Adding women and stirring does not make an equitable curriculum. For example, Anne-Marie O'Neill and Sheila Jolley (1996/1997) point out that the inclusion of food technology into the New Zealand technology education curriculum has distorted how it was taken up in the home economics curriculum, in part because home economics teachers were not invited to be part of the conversation. Food is no longer about nutrition or how to make meals or commensality and family dynamics; rather, it focuses on changes in the global expansion of production and consumption of processed foods, "enterprise culture," propelling students into the global marketplace. Connections for students with their everyday living and the home are downplayed or ignored. In the few technology education curricula elsewhere that include foods or textiles, they are presented in the context of commercial production, packaging, and marketing, with the deskilling of nutrition and food preparation.

> The model of the person involved in the pursuit of transferable marketplace skills, and the attainment of particular technological capacities is, unlike the gendered Keynesian individual...assumed to be *asocial*; neither male nor female. However the discursive underpinnings of this neoliberal model, and the essential private/public dichotomy embodied in them, reveal that this reconstituted understanding of the person and the

social relations he/she engages in, are definitely, social, cultural and gendered. (O'Neill & Jolley, 1996/1997, p. 237)

Furthermore, with an emphasis on commercial production, valuable skills learned in former sewing, cooking, craft and manual training classes are being lost.

Playing a major role in the shaping of current technology education curricula is hegemonic masculinity—*Homo technologicus*. Judy Wajcman (1991) suggests:

> The cult of masculinity which is based on physical toughness and mechanical skills is particularly strong in the shop-floor culture of working-class men. All the things that are associated with manual labour and machinery—dirt, noise, danger—are suffused with masculine qualities. Machine-related skills and physical strength are fundamental measures of masculine status and self-esteem according to this model of hegemonic masculinity. (p. 143)

Wajcman wonders whether the preoccupation with machismo and technical competence—exaggerated masculinity—is an expression of having power, or lacking power, because tradespeople are generally not in control of their jobs. However, they do have a monopoly over their tools and their machines. Chris Bastone (1995), a technology educator in British Columbia, critically reflects on the "technocratic and masculine culture" of industrial education, as well as his own enculturation to teach what was, and still is, of primary interest to tradesmen or technically inclined males.

> My technical orientation was my ontological reality and I was about to pass this "reality" on to secondary school students. At the end of the program I was "technical specialist man" qualified and initiated as "industrial education man": a teacher of the industrial young; a fraternal leader of technical enlightenment; a man of saw, blueprint, and overhead project. For me, technology was the made world—technology was a male thing. (p. 33)

Bastone discusses how he gained a more open perspective on technology, partly because of his friendship with a long-time industrial education instructor who was able to see technology beyond simply products and technical skills and was able to actualize technology as an artistic endeavour. Bastone destabilized and decentred the technical masculinity he was taught by balancing this with a more intuitive and respectful engagement with technology. Today, he works hard to not reproduce the technocratic and masculinist ideology of technology education, "softening" the hard edges of the technical of technology education in his classroom practices by engaging his students with social and cultural dimensions of technology.

Concepts such as *universal man* and *human adaptive systems* underpin and provide the impetus for technology education curriculum über/grand narratives. Universality was judged an advance over views that explicitly placed women and people from non-European cultures at a lower order, species, phylum than white males; however, feminists in their struggles for equity and decolonization have challenged these concepts. For Michel Foucault (Rabinow, 1984), "the universal intellectual, whose task was to speak the truth to power in the name of universal reason, justice, and humanity, is no longer a viable cultural figure" (p. 23). The jig is up. Regardless, technology education insists on perpetuating, sustaining, and prescribing universalization by creating standards for the study of technology, which do not include technologies historically associated with the domestic sphere and non-western peoples. I ask the students about the absence of females in technology education classes.

> James: They don't want to be here because they think that technology class is about building. You don't see guys in cooking and sewing. It's guys' jobs to build.
>
> Sarah: I'm the only girl! I have a goal to become an interior designer so I need to take drafting. If I didn't have a goal, I wouldn't take technology because it has an image of being so nerdy. The whole image of technology has to change. We can cut out so much of the stuff. We don't need a $2000 machine, the big fancy machines. Girls need to know that technology is more than making things. They think that it doesn't apply to what they do.

Sarah's experiences and feelings come as no surprise to me, echoing many of my own when I was the lone female student in technology education. It was not, and is not, a welcoming space for females. In an article I co-wrote with a female and male technology educator (Braundy, O'Riley, & Petrina, 2000), we provided a detailed analysis of the gendered situation in British Columbia, which is a reflection of the field at large. Statistics for 1998 and 1999 indicate that females make up only 3.2% of the technology teachers in British Columbia, males taking up 96.8%. ITEA records indicate a membership of 13.5% females. Educational technology fares no better. Based on their *Gen Tech Project,* Mary Bryson and Suzanne de Castell (1998) demonstrate that despite the British Columbia Ministry of Education's policy on gender equity, "under-representation and disciplinary 'ghettoization'" of females persists:

> Evidence from research on gender and access to, and uses of, new information technologies (NIT's) indicates that in public schools, female staff and students (in comparison to male students) are: (a) disenfranchised with respect to access and kind of usage, (b) less likely to acquire technological competence, and (c) likely to be discouraged from assuming a leadership role in this domain. (p. 5)

Gaining entry is the easy part. Survival in this male-dominated terrain is another matter and is taken up in a variety of complex ways. Some females (students and teachers) feel that for their own sanity they need to become "one of the boys." Others try to walk the middle ground, compromising much of who they are in their worlds outside of technology education. Those of us who want to do technology education on our own terms as females pay a very high price.

A multiplicity of exclusionary practices has contributed to the mapping of women on the periphery or as invisible in technology stories, including the assignment of women to the private sphere since the Industrial Revolution, the gendering of work and tools, and the omission of women's perspectives and contributions to technology in historical records. Representations of technology have historically been "devices, machinery, and processes which men are interested in" (Kramarae, 1988, p. 5), which is clearly reflected in technology curricula around the world. Many inventions designed by women, or for women, have been overlooked altogether because they are not considered to be technology—they are languaged as crafts or implements. Ruth Swartz Cowan (1979) underscores this point with her discussion about a baby bottle, "a simple implement...which has transformed a fundamental experience for vast numbers of infants and mothers, and been one of the more controversial exports of Western technology to underdeveloped countries—yet it finds no place in our histories of technology" (p. 52). Technologies and technological issues that are familiar and important to me such as sewing, designing leaded glass windows, weaving, nutrition, organic gardening, permaculture, and affordable community housing were nowhere in the shops filled with heavy industrial equipment, their electronic upgrades, or in the teachings within the shop/lab walls.

Many new technologies represent powerful socioeconomic and political instruments of control over women (Duelli Klein, 1987). Faulkner and Arnold (1985), Leto (1988), and Wajcman (1991) document how technologies have been used as a "social tool" to both construct and maintain stereotypical gender roles. For example, household technologies have been a significant market for manufacturers who have a monetary interest in reinforcing ideologies of gender, which is further complicated by women's complex and contradictory embrace of particular technologies. Communication technologies, automation, and robotics are often used as technologies of power and surveillance to monitor and control predominantly female workers, as they "keep an eye on her nimble fingers" (Garson, 1988; Fuentes & Ehrenreich, 1988). These technologies make possible the new "homework economy, outside the home" (Haraway, 1991c) where poor, primarily nonwhite, women work for slave wages, under slave working conditions, in transnational electronics assembly plants in the maquiladoras between Mexico and the United States, as well as other free-trade corridors in economically poor countries around the world.

The new biotechnologies are wiring people, especially women, to the integrated circuit—"microelectronics mediates the translations of labour into robotics and word processing, sex into genetic engineering and reproductive technologies, and mind into artificial intelligence and decisions procedures" (Haraway, 1991c, p. 165). Although women produce more than half of the world's subsistence food, their work remains labour intensive, whereas men's production processes benefit significantly from high tech. Some feminist researchers consider biotechnologies to be at the core of women's status, with women's bodies increasingly becoming colonized by these new technologies. When intersected by gender, race, and socioeconomics, biotechnologies take on other dimensions.

Reproductive technologies have large consequences for women within the corporate global system of production/reproduction. Women in poorer countries are often used as guinea pigs in the experimentation and testing of contraceptives, drugs, reproductive technologies and techniques that are restricted or banned in western countries until they are considered acceptable for consumption and practice on white women. Added to this are the influences of massive evangelical crusades to impose western values on indigenous women about birthing techniques and birth control, as well as the downplaying of breast feeding in favour of infant formulae and other western commodities. Women are increasingly becoming baby factories—poorer women renting their wombs to the privileged.

The new biotechnologies are inscribing more than women's bodies. Billions of dollars are being allocated for high tech, militarized, biotechnology projects to code our imperfect human bodies for retrieval as perfected genetic mutations. With the current emphasis on nationalism and global competitiveness, there are increasing political and corporate demands for "productive and efficient human resources"—frighteningly the same rhetoric as used in technology education curriculum narratives. Regardless, Wells (1995), a technology educator concerned about "confusion" around understandings of biotechnologies, argues that they are "far too inclusive, and by definition inaccurate" (p. 11). He presents an instrumental, largely economic taxonometric structure of eight biotechnologies for consideration by technology educators. Although genetic engineering has a place in his structure, reproductive technologies are absent. From my positioning as a mother, as a grandmother, as a woman, as a former inspector of workplaces, and as someone who desires social justice for all peoples, I believe that biotechnology needs to move outside of global capitalist discourses so that there can be a critical conversation on producing bodies (human resources), reproducing bodies (reproductive technologies), and bodies as commodities (gene pool).

Virtual Silence on Environment

The interrelationship between technology and the environment is rarely addressed in technology education. There would be no technology without the environment. However, environmental concerns play a negligible part of the conversation in the design and making focus of technology education.

Bruce: We have these big CocaCola companies and car companies who are pushing us to buy all these things. They shove it in our face to buy and throw it away. Everything is disposable. We need to think less about space technologies and more about recycling and responsible technologies to fix up the mess we've made.

Tony: The emphasis on the making in technology education teaches us to make more stuff. Look at all the stuff on the market that we don't need.

Bruce: We need talk about the environment to be part of technology education. Instead of sitting in technology education and making a box or something that shoots balls, talk about this too. The projects mean nothing to most kids. The projects waste wood. I will never make a catapult thing again in my life. We are not attacking castles anymore.

Gene: We need to start this at kindergarten, not at grades 11 and 12. We need to know about pollution in technology, more about recycling, using products that are biodegradable. The earth can't take it anymore. We have lots of stuff. Huge garbage dumps full.

Fabio: If we talked about the environment it would slow us down a lot.

Regardless of the vacuity in their curriculum, the students are well aware of the relationship between technology and the environment, as well as the irrelevance of many of their technology projects and their contribution to pollution and waste. Unlike the curriculum writers, they realize that environmentally sensitive protocols need to be at the centre, rather than the periphery, of the everyday practices of technology education.

How environmental issues are taught, or not taught, in schools, varies from country to country. In Australia, environmental education is a curriculum area, whereas in New Zealand, there is no environmental curriculum—technology education was chosen to be a new area of the curriculum over environmental education. In Canada, environmental education is in its infancy, in most cases as environment-across-the-curriculum, which means that it is up to a teacher to incorporate environmental practices into the classroom—or not. In British Columbia, there is a small flicker of hope for an environmental conversation being integral to technology education. In the sample theme area of "consumerism" in the British Columbia *Environmental Concepts in the Classroom: A Guide for Teachers* (1995a), there is space to consider the distinction between needs and wants, evaluation of technological solutions to specific environmental concerns, analysis of the commercial production and marketing of technology, and exploration of ethical implications of research analysis and choices made by investment corporations. However, considering the many "mays" and "mights" in the document, *if* and *how* environmental issues/practices are taken up at all in technology education depends entirely on the environmental sensitivity and resourcefulness of the particular teacher. "Sustainability" is a major theme in the document despite extensive debates questioning the meaning of sustainability. The yeah side saw it as a good word and concept, whereas the nay side saw it as little more than maintenance of the status quo. The phrase "education *about* the environment" was seen by the latter group to perpetuate the dualism between nature and culture. Annette Gough (1997) has written extensively on the politics of incorporating environmental education into school curricula. She points out that having a subject called environmental education does not mean that environmental issues are dealt with in any substantive way. Gough is concerned that the environment has become secondary to studying *about* the environment, rather than engaging *with* the environment. She urges educators to consider a more feminist poststructural approach, which she believes would situate the environment on a more equal footing with humans.

Silence on the environmental in technology education is a political act. Taking the environment seriously would interrupt the emphasis on production and consumption. By not taking heed of the current state of the environment, Noel Gough (1994b) argues that educators are "playing at ecopolitical catastrophe" as we remain (dis)engaged "in our hyper-protected society...where life is excessively easy" (p. 190). Creating a culture/environment/technology conversation is not an easy task. What counts as nature, culture, and environment in urbanized societies in particular is ambiguous and entangled with different notions of subjectivity, geography, and technology. Gough advises educators to come to terms with this "narrative complexity."

As Vizenor's story below suggests, there are devastating consequences for living too much in our heads, in words, indoors, in cyberrealities, and ignoring the language of the land:

> The abandoned earth was overtaxed with words, choking knowledge, and with no living ear on it to listen into the cold, and the animals and birds escaped to the city'....Even here, the wordies have overtaxed the cities with too much eye and not enough ears.
> The wordies lost their connections with the earth....Wordies have forgotten how to hear and when to surrender to nature and their stories.
> Electronic church bells sounded in the distance. The crow bounded on the bench and spread her feathers. The great river runs past the cities like a sewer, and the wordies hear nothing but dead voices at the university. (Vizenor, 1992, p. 132)

Te(a)ching Us and Them

Western technologies affect billions of people, most of whom have little say in their design and use. Technology education curricula pay little attention to the fact that overdevelopment in the West is at the expense of the rest of the world. However, with western privilege comes responsibility. Rather than using technology education as a place to encourage social and economic justice for all peoples, it is used to demarcate us and them—us being superior. Epistemologies and technologies that are unseen because they are positioned outside of Eurocentric blinders are portrayed as nonexistent or *pre*historic, not much use to the West, thus further fostering imperialism's claim to what it means to be educated, modern, and civilized.

Rural workers around the world, particularly Indigenous women, have been forced off their land and pushed into factories by transnational agribusiness corporations that have displaced indigenous ways of life and replaced diversity of crops with monocrops requiring the "latest piece of machinery which may render her labour obsolete, ineffective or more difficult: or with pesticides which endanger her (and her unborn) or her family" (Third World Network, 1993, p. 499). The North relies on the exploitation of workers of the South to work at slave wages in free trade zones and maquiladoras to keep labour costs down. According to Rodney Bobiwash of the Mississauga First Nation in

Canada, some of the worst human rights violations, unsafe working conditions, and environmental degradations are along the US–Mexican border, especially in Ciudad Juarez. As a former provincial factory inspector, I have witnessed deplorable working conditions of garment workers, knitting women, and farm workers in British Columbia, consisting mostly of Asian people. Bobiwash (2001) writes of the Fourth World, which is not only over there but right here at home:

> The Fourth World is…the world of Indigenous people—the original peoples of the Americas and across the globe who have been marginalized on their own lands, excluded from civil society, denied economic opportunity, and stigmatized by the Myth of Conquest and The Doctrine of Discovery—who have fallen off of even the lowest rungs of the false ladder of economic determinism—called progress. (p. 12)

Karl Grossman (1993) maintains that the discriminatory practices of dealing with toxic waste and toxic by-products of industrial and technological development amount to no less than "environmental racism"—toxic waste dumps are located in or near inner cities, radioactive contaminants are dumped on Native American reservations and First Nations reserves, Hispanic farm workers develop high incidences of pesticide-related cancers, inner city children develop lead poisoning, and toxic waste is exported to nonwestern countries; not to mention flooding of Indigenous lands for hydroelectric projects, and running high-tension lines through reserves.

Western narrative configurations ignore altogether, or portray as antiquated or primitive because of their simplicity, technologies that fall outside a mechanical model of reality, as well as technologies associated with nonwestern cultures because they do not allow for cheap, fast production—assembly-line mentality. Westernized technology discourses generally consider technologies prehistoric if they are pre- or proto- or non-Euro-American. There is little recognition that a mechanistic view of the world is simply a western knowledge project, and that other cultures' more organic ways of viewing the world, as well as their technologies, are equally valid, though their environmental sensitivity gets in the way of profit/ability. They are seen as hopelessly backward and too slow in a competitive globalized capital hyper-system.

Needham (1993) writes that although Chinese, Indian, and European-Semitic are three of the greatest historical civilizations in the world, only recently has attention been paid to their technologies and sciences. What of extra- or alloliterate societies?

While Western education purports to generate global knowledge, for all and "all around the world" (Gough, 1998), in actuality it is the economic interests of developed countries, which are reflected in education "obscuring the exploitation, domination, and social and political inequities underlying global environmental degradation" (p. 511).

> If global warming is understood as a problem for *all* of the world's peoples, then we need to find ways in which all the world's knowledge systems—Western, Blackfoot, Islam, and the like—can jointly produce appropriate understandings and responses....I am prepared to assert that a coexistence of knowledge systems is unlikely to be facilitated by the adherents of any one system arbitrarily privileging their own criteria...and therefore laying claim to producing "universal truth regardless of context." (p. 511)

Archaeologists, historians, and linguists are finally acknowledging that Aboriginal Peoples have been here in Canada for at least 15,000 years and in Australia for well over 40,000 years, long before the settler crowd. Aboriginal Peoples lived *with/as* nature. Despite centuries of colonialist efforts to eradicate their relationship with the land, and despite volumes of academic writing suggesting that these relationships have all but disappeared, many of these knowings and practices are still alive. Piracy of Indigenous knowledges and practices, medicines, and genomes has become the new frontier for pharmaceutical and agribusiness corporations who have pushed for a reinterpretation of intellectual property, permitting private ownership rights (Benjamin, 1997), as well as threatening cultural diversity and Indigenous survival. The DNA of Aboriginal and Indigenous Peoples has been 'discovered' and patented by transnational corporations. It was put forward at the United Nations Convention on Biodiversity at the Earth Summit held in Rio de Janeiro, Brazil, in 1992, that the survival of Indigenous knowledge systems might mean the survival of the earth. Perhaps this may have contributed to one of the latest neocolonial projects of discovery western academics are madly pursuing—TEK (traditional ecological knowledges), Aboriginal knowledges, methodologies, and technologies.

Interrupting Neocolonialism

The technology education students and myself are joined by Dr. mutindi ndunda, who takes time out of her very busy life to talk with us about the technologies of her community, the Mkamba from Kilome, Kenya. She shares with us how western development and technology have invaded her homeland and created immense hardships for the lives of the women in particular in Kithumba and Kyandue villages and Salama town in the Kilome Division. mutindi gives us a brief overview of her own work with her community, which looks at women's perceptions of the current state of education in Kenya for girls (Kiluva-Ndunda, 2001; ndunda, 1995). mutindi is committed to women's liberation and justice because Indigenous women's voices have been essentially silenced since the time of colonial rule. Her work makes visible the harsh social, economic, and political climate, particularly for the women in Kenya because they are not allowed to own land under the current political regime. Before the colonial regime, the land belonged to the entire clan. Since colonial rule, ownership of the land can only be registered in the names of the men. The possibility of land ownership for women is being even further eroded under the current neocolonial regime. The little land that the husbands do own is gradually being taken over by government and multinational corporations to grow coffee and other cash crops to service Kenya's huge debts to the International Monetary Fund and the World Bank. These debts were incurred through colonial restructuring of an Indigenous way of life to meet imposed western conceptions of market and political reality. These practices have drastically reduced the amount of land available to communities to grow and harvest their staple and traditional foods such as beans and maize, as well as poisoning the land with pesticides and other agribusiness technologies. mutindi tells us how women of her community are the ones who must meet the high labour demands of growing coffee, even though the coffee is registered in the name of the husband. She talks about how the health of the women of Kilome District is impacted profoundly with the increasing intensification of women's labour, yet there are few medical facilities and most women cannot afford the few medicines that are available. Many of the women she worked with were physically ill, having severe lower back and leg pains from the long hours of planting, picking, weeding, carrying, and watering. Some of the women are very young, still girls, who move to the town of Salama to try to earn a living as vegetable sellers, barmaids, and prostitutes. Salama is on the main truck route between Nairobi and Mombasa, the AIDS corridor of Africa.

mutindi spreads out a beautiful *leso*, a brightly coloured square cloth made from native materials and dyes. She reads the writings around the border.

> mutindi: This is technology

Some students roll their eyes, some laugh. mutindi demonstrates how the leso can be worn as a skirt or as a dress, or wrapped to carry things on your head, or used as a baby carrier.

> mutindi: What does the silence mean? If I came to your house, how would you feel if I treated you this way?

More silence. mutindi holds up a flyer from a local drugstore, which has advertisements for such things as deodorant, nail polish, shaving cream, toaster ovens, and hairdryers.

> mutindi: Do you think that you might be able to do without these items?
> Gene: We have never been told, "Don't do this, and don't buy that." If it's cool and we want it then we go out and buy it.
> mutindi: Is there anything wrong with your just buying and accumulating things? Can we keep doing this—buying?
> Justin: If you are working hard for your money, why shouldn't you get what you want? We get a reward for working hard. If you have food then you can get what you want with your money.
> Fabio: Here we kind of expect to have dinner every night. There you work to get a meal and stuff. Here we don't think of food and a place to live, so we get what we want on the drop of a hat.
> James: I think it is different for each society. It shouldn't be, but it is.
> mutindi: Why is it?
> James: Nobody wants to change it. It is easier to remain the way we are.
> mutindi: Why are you laughing?

The student who is laughing asks mutindi what the boys their age do for fun in her village. mutindi explains that fun is not separated from the tasks of everyday life in her community as it is in western cultures. She gives an example of herding the goats as something that the boys in her village enjoy doing. The goats are their friends. The community, including the younger ones, also enjoy listening to the "old ones" tell stories because of their importance to the education of the community through the passing on of traditional knowledge from generation to generation. mutindi tells the students that the community feels a great loss when a storyteller dies; it is like a library burning down.

> mutindi: What about the environment? Can we keep buying and throwing things out and getting new ones?
> Paul: If we work and can afford things, why should we buy things for them, and do everything for them? Then they don't have to worry about getting a job.
> James: If you lived in Kenya and you got extra money—I don't know how you would get it—you would probably buy a big house. Right?
> mutindi: I don't need a big house. If I had extra money I would start a bank. I told you about these women I'm working with from Kenya. These women work very hard, very long days, and they only end up with about $10 to $50 Canadian at the end of each month. What they are trying to do is trade vegetables, take them to the market, and get a profit of another $1 or $2, and then save it so that they can buy food. You want to support people so that they can support themselves. Why is it that they are poor? That is a big question.
> James: That's because you're following western ways. The natives here didn't build big houses like we do.

By situating western technologies as the default position in technology education curricula, students are not only learning that western technologies are superior, they are also missing out on learning about the technologies that have been around for tens of thousands of years throughout this hemisphere. For example, learning from Lower Stl'atl'imx and Lil'wat communities about their traditional housing might encourage students to rethink western housing practices, in particular community housing and sustainable materials and techniques. The Lower Stl'atl'imx, for example, built ten to twenty metre long square and oblong communal houses made of logs and cedar planks, called *ishkin*, which accommodated four to eight families (Hudson & DePaoli, 1999; Wright, 1999). These buildings stood for many thousands of years far outliving homes built in Canada since the time of colonization, especially the poorly designed and shoddily constructed homes built by the Ministry of Indian and Northern Affairs on First Nations reserves across Canada. Students might examine the possibilities of co-operative housing in their own neighbourhoods that would be affordable, ecological, built by the local community, and made of local materials to last for centuries rather than decades.

mutindi: Our houses are made of mud with thatched roofs, mud with corrugated iron-sheets or bricks with corrugated iron-sheets. They last a long time, and they can trap the water because we don't have plumbing.
Derek: You're trying to become western because that house is not a hut.
Rob: If you're trying to become western then you need to buy and sell. Those materials just don't appear.
mutindi: You've forgotten Kenya is a colonized country. You're forgetting that white people came there and established their own multinationals there. They started their own companies to sell these products. It is not that we are trying to become western; these things were brought to us, and we were actually forced to buy these things.
Rob: How can you be forced to do anything?
mutindi: Western society comes and says, "This is what it means to be modern," and because you are powerful you begin to build these houses and you begin to sell this kind of thing. And you give these people some little education and whatever it means to be modern is what looks like white.
Derek: You don't say, "Hey, this is white." You know it came from us, the West. So, it must be modern.
mutindi: What is being modern now? Who are 'us'? Did you know the White House was built by black slaves? Whose sweat has this country been made of? First Nations people were here and supported people who came in. And, what happened to them? Their land was taken and they were killed. I'm glad we're talking about these things—us and them.

The students have learned distinctions between contemporary western technologies in order to demarcate communities of us and them. Aboriginal and Indigenous Peoples have not been part of the conversation in technology education; rather they are viewed as *pre*-historic or *extra*-historic, because theirs was not primarily an orthographically literate society. History has come to mean only the written word. "Ecological societies, or other societies based on more constant time, low technologies, and various archaisms...are thought to be hopelessly 'backward'...in relation to an international capitalist system" (Conley, 1993, p. 82). Aboriginal technologies are dismissed or trivialized in technology education curricula. For example, in the British Columbia curriculum, a reference to First Nations is in a sample project in which students are to carve totem poles. For Peter Cole (2000a), such tokenized appropriation and reproduction of First Nations art forms shows disrespect for First Nations knowledges and practices. Furthermore, he warns that westerners do not understand what they are catching when they hang dreamcatchers in their cars or homes or offices.

> white people sell sweetgrass
> dreamcatchers eaglefeathers medicine bags you name it
> they got it or can get it
> in taiwan hongkong japan formosa indonesia ko rea
> those newager highwager trinketizer whities
> dishonour the indian people whose land they stole
> hey monias wanna buy some authentic ated First Nations poop
> midden locally hooo you got that one good
> so whydon'tchatakedown all that stuff
> about my culture off your walls and shelves and tables
> and display boards and sell your own how about that
> oh you don't hmmmmm (p. 112)

Unless the teachers of the totem pole carving are First Nations carvers from that particular community, this will be yet another example of appropriation and ahistorical, acontextual misrepresentation. How else would the students know which tree to choose? What prayers and medicines to offer for thanks? How to take the tree down? How it is to be transported? The history, story, and ownership of the design? Whether permission has been granted to use a particular design? Where the totem pole is to be erected, and the protocols involved? There is no place in this academic colonization for First Nations to dispute such tokenization, to tell their own stories, and to share their traditional practices. Students are required to legitimate the monoculture and disciplinary assumptions of the world as imagined from within Eurocentric parameters.

Although a few of the students in our discussion express outright indifference to those less advantaged, as well as to mutindi, there is a range of responses from denial to blaming.

> Rob: There is a difference though, right, between us and them because we live in this kind of society, and they live in Africa. We never talk about them.
> mutindi: Have you ever thought about why it is that it is so restricted in Africa, and yet here we have so much?
> Mike: Population.
> mutindi: You think it is population?
> Mike: That's what we learn.
> mutindi: I don't know what kind of history you are reading. I'm going to be honest. You read what you want to read. You hear what you want to hear. Here I am telling you exactly what is happening in Kenya and you don't want to hear.
> James: Nobody wants to change it. It is easier to remain the way we are.
> Justin: We have enough problems here; we don't need to think about them.

A first response for some students is that they do not want to know. They are very uneasy. mutindi anticipates their resistance to what is different from their own embodied knowings. As Willinsky (1998) points out, "in attempting to find a way beyond colonized forms of knowledge, one has to be careful not to imagine that they invariably colonize the learner. Students can and do turn to their own advantage what they are taught" (p. 109). mutindi tells the students that she hopes that this first hand sharing of what is going on in her community may encourage them to do things differently in their own lives so that the divide between us and them disappears.

After mutindi has gone home, we talk about what they may have learned from mutindi's time with them. We discuss how students are bombarded with images of bombs, homeless people, starving and dying children on a daily basis on television, movies, video games, and the Internet. It is much easier to learn about others less fortunate when filtered through a video screen and the voice of a dispassionate, most often white, narrator. They experienced mutindi not as a docu-genre voiceover with the appropriate timbre, such as that on the Discovery channel, at the National Film Board of Canada, and Channel 4 on the British Broadcasting Corporation, with accompanying exotic and sensationalized film footage. mutindi brought her uncensored and unsanitized concerns into the technology education classroom, in her *coloured* flesh, with breath, passion, caring, anger, and humour. The students came face-to-face with an 'other' reality and they did not have the technology to tune out and/or flip to another channel. They all had the option to leave at any time. They all chose to stay.

On a different plateau in another time and space, the students gave some thought to mutindi's sharing of her story with them:

Fabio: mutindi really opened my eyes to things I had never thought of before.

Justin: Of course, we use these places to our advantage. They don't grow what they need, the corn and potatoes, because we want our coffee beans. We never think about how this affects their way of life.

Fabio: I always thought of technology as computers. After mutindi, I thought more than just electronics, computers, graphics, spaceships.

Justin: Now I think differently. I sort of knew before, having things produced in other countries, having them take the garbage end of the deal, the workers, and effluent from all the plants, the crap. Our technology definitely affects other people.

Several students asked if mutindi could come back to speak with them again. One student felt that it is the responsibility of mutindi and those marked as 'other' to educate them, while other students began to realize that we are all related, and we all need to take responsibility for our thoughts and actions.

Knotting Columbus

It should come as no surprise that the stories of technology as articulated by the "heirs of Columbus" (Vizenor, 1991) might get all knotted up in rhizomes and trickster discourse in a different tail/tale s/pinning. As Gerald Vizenor points out, Columbus made appearances through his manifest manners, not only as "that third person discoverer of mother earth," but also as "the deverbative trickster, the one who landed in two pronouns, the he and you; the understudies of mother earth" (Vizenor, 1994a, p. 107). Columbus inadvertently lands on this plateau with a little assistance from Old Coyote in her dancetelling of *A Coyote Columbus Story* (King, 1993).

> Boy, that Coyote is a silly Coyote. You got to watch out for her. Some of Coyote's stories have got Coyote tails and some of Coyote's stories are covered in scraggy Coyote fur but all of Coyote's stories are bent.
> Christopher Columbus didn't find America....Christopher didn't find Indians, either. You got a tail on that story. (p. 121)
> But if Christopher Columbus didn't find America and he didn't find Indians, who found those things?
> Those things were never lost, I says. Those things were always here. Those things are still here today. (p. 127)

Old Coyote's retelling of such a taken-for-granted story in education, playfully encourages the students to look critically at the story of technology they are learning. The students are asked to think about who gets to create the dominant story of technology; what and whose technologies are in/out; what might technology stories look like if they were created from different perspectives and life experiences; and how is the masculine-technical story of technology maintained in education? The hegemonic storylines get all tangled up in Old Coyote's narrative chance, unable to escape her frenzy of words. S/he disrupts the dominant storylines, makes new conjunctions, rejects standardizations, and irritates complacency. The students take delight in seeing the similarities between Old Coyote's retelling of the discovery of America, and the *one true story* they are being told about technology in school.

> Bruce: The Coyote story made me think that we need more ways of looking at things.
> Justin: Coyote makes us think of the people part of technology. We just do the assignments and don't think about anything else. Most students wouldn't want to think about this; they would want to just do the project.
> Fabio: We are told that the story changes each time a government changes, like in Russia and the United States. And here too. The propaganda by the governments—I thought of that when you read the Coyote story.

> Tony: I see Coyote like technology. It is good and bad. Our technology is bad for mutindi, but it is good for us.

Teaching technology as a space of narrative chance, rather than a ceaseless questing for standardizations and more-better-faster, allows students opportunities to get in touch with and free their own imagination, their own bodies and spirits. Most of the students believe that their schooling has let them down, and they feel strongly that they have a right to know how the space of difference between us and those less economically advantaged was created, what is in the between-space, and how that space might become more reciprocal and shared.

> Fabio: That's not our fault that we don't know these things. We don't learn that in school.
> Bruce: We need to understand what we are doing around the world instead of saying what we do in Canada doesn't affect the rest of the world.
> Gene: We need to hear this more in school. Why aren't teachers telling us these things?

Writing about science education curriculum, specifically, Willinsky (1998) argues that a curriculum that "obscures the discipline's contributions to the meaning of race is incomplete and irresponsible" (p. 187). The same holds true for technology education and any other curriculum area. Further, Willinsky contends that students have a right to know that the exclusion of other is "not simply an oversight but a feature of how the disciplines...have gone about dividing the world since the age of the empire" (p. 250).

> Sarah: We need someone to ask questions to. Instead we just go numb, like a vegetable sitting in front of a machine. We need more classes that put our brain and feelings together.
> James: Teachers don't want us to critique. Dialoguing in a class is new for me, talking about my education. Sometimes it is so hard to sit there. A teacher would take offense to questioning. They say, "That is just the way it is." Teachers don't know how to do this. It is not their fault. It is as far as they go, so it is like go away.

Sadly, the students feel their teachers are unable to deliver. What a powerful and telling ironic twist, particularly since many of these technology education students are deemed to be less academically inclined than many of their peers.

Prescribed curricula shortchange students in other ways. They neglect and dismiss the richness and diversity of knowledges and experiences the students already have. Students' understandings of technology are informed largely by texts outside of school, including their family, their culture, their experiences, their jobs, television, videos, movies, computer games, comic books, magazines, music, body language. "Students have a right to see what the West, and its proud process of education, has made of them, even as this knowledge is bound to complicate and implicate their education" (Willinsky, 1998, p. 246). Students need to be introduced "to the fragile nature of truth, to the moral dimensions of this inquiry, and to the responsibilities we have as practitioners and students....[in order] to propose an education concerned with the historical dimensions of universal truths" (p. 187). It is important for them to know how the "truths" of their curriculum were constructed and how they benefited the dying profession of industrial arts/crafts teacher who appropriated the word *technology* to advance and empower him/her/self. Students might then learn how the West divided the world to its advantage, basing the divisions on a technological basis (high = us; low/no = them). The challenge is to get gender, culture, socioeconomics, and environment into technology education, and to get sexism, racism, capitalism, and all the other -isms out.

It has been a long day. I will have to paddle fast to reach my campsite on the other side of the lake before night falls. I thought I saw Coyote, or was that a cedar branch wavering in the last light?

Virtual(ly) Ed Tech

> The spread of computers in every aspect of life is not only accelerating the commodification process, which now includes the genetic basis of life processes, but is also reinforcing a form of rootless individual subjectivity which finds fulfillment through endless consumerism and technological innovation.
> —Chet Bowers, *Toward a Cultural and Ecological Understanding of Curriculum*

> I don't need a computer   I got a pen   and when
> that runs out   I got a knife and lots of pencils
> my kid's crayons   charcoal   lots of hardware anyway I
> got no 'lectricity in my shack like most of us
> —Peter Cole & Patricia O'Riley, *Much Rezadieu about (Dewey's) Goats in the Curriculum*

Exhausted I lie down to rest on the soft moss near the water; listen to the waves, the wind. Just when I think I am away from it all, I awaken to the distant din of civilization on the prowl: trucks, deforesting equipment, unearthing equipment, and digital noise. This plateau has been invaded by dot com, dot org, dot edu, dot world. This plateau has been leased to corp.world@everywhere.dev. They're bringing container loads of high tech everything up by helicopter. The dust and clang of roadbuilding are getting nearer. Won't be long before this place is crawling with opportunity. Screens everywhere. Wires. Wirelesses. Keyboards. Dishes. Connectivity. The last plateau was the hardwiring; this one is the virtualizing, the interiorizing. Mirrors inside, mirrors outside. Lots of opportunity for reflection. Putting the machines into us, us into the machines. Becoming unbecoming. This plateau is overrun with modern frenzy, hyperactivity to the nth degree. The attention deficit syndrome of the baby boomers has become a full-blown disease, infecting not only their children and grandchildren, but even their own parents. People are frantic to get away from it, but there are no drugs that work, no book that works, no channel that works, no guru. No instant lottery.

People are becoming digitized but some life on this plateau is resisting. From here, you can see human beings enter a wired world, a high tech space of surface/screen, virtual communication, subminiaturization, and sociotechnical production of texts, bodies, and geographies. Written into the surface of this plateau are inscriptions, *dys*-scriptions, and dematerializing (un)realities in virtual space and time. The incomers dys-identify, dys-semble, dys-morph, as they pass through the screen. Hoping I will be able to come back whole, I also choose to enter, hoping I can learn to act as a guide for those who come after. The hazards of physicality are left behind, as we morph into cybersubjectivities. There is no need for under/over/foot/wear, only software for this part of the journey. Plug in, recline, inhabit—the multisited global network, where embodiments and articulations implode and are reconstituted as collaboratively made hyperrealities and hypertextualities.

I left my copy of this plateau on my desk overnight and awoke to Coyote's editing marks, which I include. I am reminded of the children's story about a shoemaker (and his wife) who were struggling with their business until the little people started helping them, coming each night and fixing the shoes. I wonder if Coyote read that story. Maybe I should leave my shoes out, too. If I leave the remaining plateaux out, as well as the first six, maybe s/he will add her/his own commentary. Coyote leaves no quotation marks when s/he speaks, no punctuation marks, no capitals, unless s/he wants to.

> *if Columbus had discovered the digital/cyborg world instead of the 'new world'   maybe we'd still have our homeland   and natives*

From the privileged position of cyberspace, new potentialities and holographic fields of play can remake humanity and the universe. This space can be used to wage collective struggles against injustice, including global corporate capitalism, a new form of colonization that renders virtually invisible the wetware and other resources used to produce hyperrealities, as well as realizing exhilarating simulacra of other and metamorphizing fantasies. Most of the world cannot pay the high price to enter this virtual space. However, they are paying it anyway, and will, well into the future. The majority of people are just trying to feed, clothe, and house themselves—and overcome the effects of centuries of empirization, monarchization, industrialization, mercantilization, exploration, and other kinds of colonization, genocide, global holocaustization. As the song goes, "Money makes di vorl' go roun' it's clinking clanking sound."

> *would that be the sound of coins or bills   I think not   more like the sound of plastic   the sound of keyboards   creating   buying   transferring   forging   wealth*

Cyborgology

> For some time now there has been a rumor going around that the age of the human has given way to the posthuman. Not that humans have died out, but that the human as a concept has been succeeded by its evolutionary heir. Humans are not the end of the line. Beyond them looms the cyborg, a hybrid species created by crossing biological organism with cybernetic mechanism....From the beginning it is constructed, a technological object, that confounds the dichotomy between natural and unnatural, made and born. (Hayles, 1995, p. 321)

Humans have always had a relationship with technologies. This relationship has been intensified over the past decades with computer technologies altering our senses and becoming part of human ontologies. As Donna Haraway (1991c) writes, an "informatics of domination" has shifted an "organic industrial society to a polymorphous information system" (p. 161), which has already transformed our bodies into cyborgs—part human, part machine. In western society especially, the biological human is giving way to a more technical human and evolving into what N. Katherine Hayles refers to as a posthuman. The push to clone humans may create post-posthumans.

The supersaturation of *techno*thinking and *techno*practices that permeate present-day western education contribute to the docility of student bodies and their receptivity to the hypertextual language of science and technology. This "State apparatus" (Deleuze & Guattari, 1987) is all about control, regulation, and hierarchical structures, resonating with Michel Foucault's (1979, 1980) "technologies of the self" and "technologies of normalization." With the increasing prominence of computer and multimedia technologies in education as predominant learning or support technologies, educators need more than ever to pay attention to the semiotic, material, and social flows, as well as their implications for pedagogy and curriculum. Rather than rushing blindly headlong to get high (teched), educators need to slow down a bit, breathe, and take the time to carefully consider ways to converse with "this world-as-code a high-tech military field, a kind of automated academic battlefield, where blips of light called players disintegrate (what a metaphor!) each other in order to stay in the knowledge and power game" (Haraway, 1991c p. 185). Haraway (1991b) argues that we need to make alliances with those who practice "in the belly of a heavily militarized, communications-system-based technoscience in its late capitalist and imperialist forms" (p. 6).

Haraway enlivens dialogue within western metaphysics, eschewing the opposition between nature and culture, real and artificial. In order to do this, she advocates the use of metaphors such as cyborg and trickster/Coyote that "show us that historically specific human relations with 'nature' must somehow—linguistically, scientifically, ethically, politically, technologically, and epistemologically—be imagined as genuinely social and actively relational" (1991b, p. 21). Shh! Here comes a *Canis* latrans formation.

> trickster/Coyote?   she hasn't asked me or any of my Coyote relations for permission to turn us into a metaphor   what's a metaphor?

Rather than resist postmodern capitalism and its cyborg culture, Haraway argues that we should embrace the subversive possibilities of cyborgian imagery, because we have no choice but to move through "artifactualism" to a geography as elsewhere.

> hmmm interesting   'we' have no choice   because...

Viewing global sisterhood projects, common interest alliances, and appeals to anti-technological, organic naturalist, and essentialist body wholeness a waste of energies and time, Haraway invites us to consider a new politics that would unfold "partial, contradictory, permanently unclosed constructions of personal and collective selves" (1991c, p. 157).

> *well   if she's going to be a primatologist I'm going to be a logoprimatist and study the words of the two-leggeds   anyway raven what is this desire for global alliances   global villages   when local peoples and villages are being ignored   subsumed   bypassed   in the seduction to become anamorphized into   virtual fllesh?*

The cyborg is the boundary creature, a split and contradictory self, "partial in all its guises...always constructed and stitched together imperfectly, and *therefore* able to join with another, to see together without claiming the other" (Haraway, 1991a, p. 22).

> *try living in the bush a few days and you'll soon learn about border creatures and split self and stitching together   won't be any theory involved*

Haraway (1991c) challenges her readers to consider embodied refigurative writing practices, "cyborg writing," troping and knotting together key phallocentric technoscience narrativites in the "production of worldly interference patterns" as a hope not only for survival, but also for more livable worlds. Engaging cyborg writing offers possibilities for new languages and sensibilities for remapping technology discourses in education.

> *I remember inventing   or was it discovering   the original two-legged inhabitants of this hemisphere as they now stand   and I remember them electing me trickster   but I don't remember discovering donna haraway or any of those other imports who seem to be claiming me*

> *music please   oops too late   I've already danced through the screen and back   I don't even have a usb port or tools from ikea*

Haraway suggests that "feminist cyborg stories have the task of recoding communication of intelligence to subvert command and control" (p. 175). For cyborg writing to become more than textual re-readings from privileged bodies and locations, there also needs to be *materialized reconfiguring* from the bodies and geographies of those who been trampled on in the rush to become wired —remapping curriculum narratives and classroom practices.

Cyborgs in Education

Suzanne Damarin (1994) explores how cyborg and goddess mythologies relate to the "spiral dance" of teaching, noting that teachers are always already both cyborg and goddess. She searches for a third term to the cyborg/goddess binary positionalities for teachers.

> *how about third base or short stop or midfield hoooowwwl*

The goddess myth has been placed on women for centuries, with the "continuance of mothering and nurturing of the individual child" (p. 3) being extended into the classrooms of female teachers. Notwithstanding the added political demands being placed on teachers for productivity and efficiency, the goddess myth persists and inscribes female teachers. Damarin resists the teacher as goddess myth, arguing that "teachers are...earthly creatures who must negotiate their sustenance and positionalities in the material world" (p. 5).

> *I guess you have to be human or human of a certain proclivity to understand that   with all due respect   and I mean that as it reads   unless you've been involved with a spiral in your own life   your own experience   talking about spiral dance is like talking about event horizons or the temperature of stars unless you've been there you're blowing borrowed air*

With the current push for computer technologies in/as education, Damarin points out that the teacher as goddess is now assigned "those (sub)service tasks required to establish and continue the hegemony of man-machines in the redefinition of education" (p. 7). Concerned about the lack of other than goddess role models, Damarin provides her own imaginary—cyborgian teachers. The cyborgian teacher works to "subvert the intentions of machine donor and use computers to reproduce and magnify their own personalities" and are "unfaithful to the fathers, but she does not forget what they have done" (pp. 11–12). Damarin comes up with a third term—postmodern witches, mothers, and loners—to resist and transgress the cyborg/goddess binary. A W.I.T.C.H. (Wild Independent Thinking Crone and Hag) has "transformative powers like the cyborg....[but] unlike the cyborg whose milieu is surface and boundary....the witch is at home with depth and duration" (p. 13).

> *how about coyotes   we predated witches and human language   so we didn't get caught up in two-legged talk for a long time*

The laughing teacher "dances with the children on a cyberspace dancefloor" (p. 15) and is not tied to a "worldly search for good sex" and "an income reflecting her 'comparable worth'" (p. 16), an extension of a laughing mother. The alone standing teacher is a border creature, standing/sweeping with one foot out (goddess-like) and one foot in (cyborgian). The responsibility of cyber-witch teachers is to teach children "witchcrafty sweeping, alone standing laughing, and cyborgian spellcasting" (pp. 18–19), so that they can create their own humanness as they are being constructed to be more like machines.

> *machines are the legacy human beings leave the world*

With nature increasingly becoming a technocultural construction, an artefact, Noel Gough (1993) contends that educators need to attend to the narrative complexity of such concepts as self, culture, nature, and artefact. Culture and environment are increasingly being foregrounded by "second nature" (Jameson, quoted in Gough, 1997)—the built environment of buildings, cities, roads, railroads, airports, which is even further destabilized as "third nature of information flows" (Wark, quoted in Gough, 1997).

> *those human languages are getting them in trouble filling their heads with philosophy   they need to get out and split some wood   draw some water*

Similarly, Elizabeth Grosz (1992) suggests that:

> The body and its environment....produce each other as forms of the hyperreal, as modes of simulation which have overtaken and transformed whatever reality each may have had into the image of the other: the city is made and made over into the simulacrum of the body, and the body, in its turn, is transformed, "citified," urbanized as a distinctively metropolitan body. (p. 242)

> *get away from your computer   go hiking   rough it   scavenge in 'the wild' for food   learn to hide*

For Gough (1997), the gap between the concept and materiality of cyborgs no longer exists:

> The kinds of cyborgs we and our children are now—and are possibly becoming—will be shaped by the stories we mutually construct. Furthermore, the generation and materialization of these possibilities is as much a function of textual silences, denials, and refusals, as it is of whatever may explicitly be privileged by a text. Even if we ignore cyborgs, I doubt that they will go away. (p. 76)

possibilities?   hm I wonder if they're like potentialities raven

you're asking the wrong bird   I'm only acquainted with real things like breakfast lunch and snacks

With this in mind, Gough (1993) suggests educators "need to provide students with more complex and complicating discourses; we can no longer assume to re/present, interpret, and explain 'reality' and the "complexity and instability of the phenomenal world that presents itself to human sensibilities" (p. 621). He suggests that schooling ought to be a place to deconstruct, construct and interrogate the world-as-text and to consider carefully the implications of technocultural and ecopolitical constructions of multistoried textual practices.

these two-leggeds are obsessed with texts   what about trees   what about what is written in the sky   the earth   on the waves   in dreams?

Gough envisions the constructive possibilities of engaging Haraway's cyborgian imagery in education as significant narrative experiments. He suggests that educators need to pay attention to the "machineries of texts" that construct cyborgs, not simply their hardware, but their narrativity—how they function textually and intertextually as pretexts toward digital narratives.

First World Netscape and Third World Landscape?

> Might virtual reality or computer simulation be harnessed, one wonders, for the purposes of multicultural pedagogy? . . . It would be naïve to place exaggerated faith in these new technologies, for their expense makes them exploitable mainly by corporations and the military. (Shohat & Stam, 1994, p. 356)

Virtual(ly) Ed Tech 107

Some writers are more cautious about embracing virtual con/re/figurations. For example, Elizabeth Grosz (1992) explores how notions of spatiality are affected by the technologization and technocratization of urban space. She uses the metaphor of the city-as-machine, however, not one modeled on the engine but on computer technologies that reduce distance and speed to immediate, instantaneous gratification.

> raven   *have you ever had a computer crash   ever felt even a little upset with your hardware?*
>
> no   *but I dropped an apple once*

Grosz argues that "the replacement of geographical space with the screen interface, the transformation of distance and depth into pure surface, the reduction of space to time, of the face-to-face encounter to the terminal screen" (p. 251) transforms our "mutually defining relations between corporeality and the metropolis" (p. 243). Geographical space and bodies collapse into the surface of the terminal's screen: space and bodies implode into time/instantaneous communication. Verena Andermatt Conley (1993) asks whether people are becoming "terminal humans" or "human terminals" as social links are disrupted and people are confined into "habitacles" (tiny living spaces) where they are glued to their chairs, linked by various threads and remote controls...and tuned into virtual realities" (p. 87)—both terminus and terminal.

> *if I remember my pencil writing days   much the same analogy works with the page which I guess is as geographical as a computer screen   I remember those first human beings who started writing thinking to themselves they were becoming cyborgs   the artists too   musicians afraid they'd collapse into the cave wall   the instrument   the papyrus*

Grosz (1992) reminds us that in cyberspace the body is subordinated to the mind and is merely a bridge linking a nonspatial consciousness to the material.

> *this talk of nonspatial consciousness puzzles my simple coyotic mind   a noncoyote I suppose could include a rock   a frog   a cloud   but non-spatial? would that (according to relativistic theory) mean time?   'how' is anything nonspatial?   how do we think in or to that place?   does all spatiality need*

> to be about the physical dimensions that human beings recognize or are familiar with?   as for consciousness I guess it's one of those things that scientists wish people would stop referring to because they don't know how to measure it   if space is a measure or measuring or measureable and is describa(b)ble in terms of noun-ness   if it is a tool invented by certain human beings in order to 'discover'/claim that which it represents   and if consciousness is a notion invented by human beings to account for that which cannot be measured   what exactly is grosz talking about   conceptualizations I would guess

With this implosion of time into space and "the 'cross-breeding' of the body and machine," Grosz asks, "whether the machine will take on the characteristics attributed of the human body...or whether the body will take on the characteristics of the machine?" (p. 252).

> either/or   a convenient binary   what does it take to become a machine or unbecome one?

Conley (1993) raises concerns that the exciting potential of becoming advocated by Deleuze and Guattari is being appropriated by integrated world capitalism for destructive ends and uncontrollable production of unnecessary consumer products.

> unnecessary? un-necessary hmmm?   I wonder if it's like not necessary and how can something be un- something

With Christian humanity entering a new millennium, Paul Virilio's (1993) warning has become realized: "At the end of our century not much will remain of this planet that is not only polluted and impoverished, but also shrunken and reduced to nothing by the teletechnologies of generalized interactivity" (p. 12). Neoliberal politics and hypercapitalism, have re-imaged the world into ahistorical limitless utopian views with shortened horizons and accelerated loss of physical and metaphorical space. Is there a possible exit—*sortie*? Conley writes of "mapping a practice of ecosubjectivity" based on more constant time and more sustainable technologies. For this, she joins Walter Benjamin's (1968) *storytelling*, with Deleuze and Guattari's (1987) *becoming*, as a potentiality to decompress and renarrativize our current technological condition. Storytelling and becoming do not dismiss the human machine interface; they offer potential to open space in the high tech grids for one's own body, narrative, and history in an affirmation of life.

> human/machine interface   hmmm   does that mean there's a border   border patrol   transmigration controls?

Conley's storytelling/becoming is a slowing down in the noise, stimulation, and "dromospheric pollution" (Virilio, 1999) of hyperreality that minimize/miniaturize the distances of the world, disintegrate diversity, and devastate the planet so that there may be space for breath and life and caring.

Along with minimization and miniaturization, Margaret Visser (2002) suggests that computerization, in particular the information highway, the Internet, is concerned with trivialization and belittlement, "a deliberate social strategy in which facts are reduced to insignificance" (p. 75). She cautions that this descent into meaningless, and mindlessness is not educating, but feeding our ignorance as we rely on others to do our thinking for us.

> Sometimes we seem actually to believe that "de-skilling" the population is useful: people will be quiet because they are incapable. If they are ignorant, they might even buy more! We seem to think that no consequences will follow from our neglect. Indeed, we often fail to think about it at all. (p. 78)

Although the cyborg is an important figuration to resist the dehumanizing cultural effects of the artefactualization, miniaturization, and trivialization of the world, some feminists are concerned that the cyborg may rehabilitate rather than subvert the artifice.

> The representation of femininity as artifice and/or machine is already a well-established trope in modernity existing alongside, and sometimes in conflict with, the more familiar ideal of woman as redemptive, unalienated nature. Such representations, however, seem to function less as subversive challenges to the ideology of humanism than as misogynistic fantasies of gaining final control over an unruly female body. Haraway's assumption that the appeal to artifice is more transgressive than the evocation of nature becomes questionable in the light of such history. (Felski, quoted in Goshorn, 1994, pp. 280–281)

For Hayles (1993), "our sense of our physical bodies, their capabilities and limitations, boundaries and extension, deeply informs both the objects and the codes of representation" (p. 173).

> *I guess I'm just not getting this human speech after thousands of years   I guess it wasn't actually my first language   hey raven what does 'deeply inform' mean?*
>
> *it's like when you think you buried something deep and you keep digging and you keep digging but you just put it under a leaf someplace else and you were not only digging in the wrong place but using the wrong verb*
>
> *oh? so how do you know about digging?*
>
> *I watch lots of garden shows on tv*

The merging of physical and textual bodies into actual and virtual realities joined by computer technologies "splice a human subject into a cybernetic circuit by putting the human sensorium in a direct feedback loop with computer data banks" (p. 174). In cyberspace, human sensory and cognitive habitation becomes displaced by a cybernetic construct.

Furthermore, although doing much to untie women from the goddess image and opening spaces for other possibilities, the cyborg metaphor also brings with it problems. Hayles maintains that the thrill of creating and exploring this new technosubjectivity in disembodied space consists of a better-than-life sensorium that diverts attention from the cultural forces behind the machine logic that is "the Procrustean bed into which human perception must fit" (p. 175). Those who have access to cyberspace, have the privilege to escape from the everyday difficulties of being bodily engaged in the world.

> *escape?   I'd see it more like being a dungeon or cage*

Sense, empathy, and eroticism merge as bodies dissolve and become modified and spliced into teledildonic fantasies that can provide titillation and escape. Computer constructs are more easily accessed, more sanitized, and less troublesome than messy, imperfect, unpredictable physical bodies. The escape fantasy of cyber-space worlds relieves people of and diverts them from facing the irreversible messes and problems created with technology. The will to virtuality becomes the new medical model of desire being played out in the psycho logics (O'Riley & Scott, 1996).

> **The illness/diagnosis:**
> Lacanian phantasm of holes, lacks, needs, yearnings; all humanly impossible to satisfy, if satisfaction is the game. And, it is. The scene is set for the will to virtuality.
> **The cure:**
> Technological feasting, hi-tech prosthesis. Technology as the new narcotic, injectable phallus, available to all comers, all wired heads, all genders and orientations, the fair neuterizer, the great equalizer, shooting up fictions. You can prescribe your own medication and dosage: you can arouse or tranquilize; you can go as fast as you want with no movement at all. Annihilation or survival? It is your call. (p. 105)

Hayles argues that "leaving the body behind equates to the belief that if the problems won't go away from us, perhaps we can go away from the problems" (p. 183).

> *raven what would happen if we unproblematised everything—including assumptions which have become 'truths'? what if hundreds of generations of earthworms and squirrels argued about problematizing had royal commissions on the usefulness or validity of a walnut?*
>
> *but they do this all the time they enact those troublings in their everyday lives but they don't waste time arguing about what ifs they're too busy living in their bodies living in your head can mean living in the attic and having no access to the rec room and the rest of the house*
>
> *hey raven how do I keep from problematizing unproblematizing?*
>
> *stop thinking with your head*

Participants in the high tech world of cyborgs never meet face-to-face with the actual sounds of war. Or poverty. These are unrealities, unrealized in this uncontaminated playground.

> The Cold War of hard ideology may finally be over, but the new Cold War of soft ideology, the one that pits the virtual class against all barriers to its global sovereignty, is just beginning. (Kroker & Weinstein, 1994, p. 6)

Western media constantly bomb(ard)s us with the sophistication and precision of the American military attacks on Afghanistan, now Iraq, but we seldom see the tears and hear the cries of the injured and the children of these countries. We do not hear the voices of entire villages of Indigenous peoples in Colombia who have been killed by the military and paramilitaries so that transnational mining and petroleum companies can expropriate their lands and resources.

> *no they don't call that terrorism   it's enforced capitalist prevention   like the pre-emptive strikes in vietnam   news-speak   national security   now the pre- pre-emptive strikes on iraq*

According to United Nations statistics, "despite the widely recognized benefits of globalization, more than a billion of the world's 6 billion people still cannot fulfill their basic needs for food, water, sanitation, healthcare, housing, and education" (United Nations, 2002, p. 9). Most of us do not come face-to-face with the 28,500,000 people dying of AIDS in sub-Saharan Africa. We are content to peer at exotic other, and we do peeeeer.

Hayles maintains that virtual reality gives the illusion of "connectivity, sensitivity to others' choice, open-ended creativity, freewheeling exploration" (p. 184); she argues that masculine ethics of control prevails. Cyberspace is more than a contraction of three dimensionality into the two dimensionality of surface/screen. It is a darker reconstitution of spatiality that extends into the "endo spaces of the body as well as the cyberspaces of virtual reality" (p. 185).

> *it's not a con/traction dr hayles   it's a sub/traction   three minus one or maybe some kind of fancy square rooting multiplied by a logorithm or a variable   a contraction is when the other dimension is retrievable   and my limited understanding is that you can't unstuff what's not in there*

As gendered patterns of concavity and convexity move through the surface of the screen, they become more arbitrary, subject to rearrangements and reassemblies that are bound by informational rather than physical constraints...the fictional worlds of cyberspace are replete with androgynous figures....the Other is either assimilated into the self to become an inferior version of the Same or remains outside as a threatening and incomprehensible alterity. So women are constructed as castrated men or

Medusa figures; blacks as inferior whites or cannibalistic devils; the poor as lazy indigents or feral criminals. (pp. 187–188)

hey raven   not to mention aboriginal peoples as genetic mutants

and coyotes and ravens as textual deviants

Hayles suggests that we take seriously the metaphor of colonization, as well as the seduction of cyberspace. She does not advocate abandoning cyberworlds as they can open up new vistas; however, she asks that we look at the underside of the seductive powers of cyborg imagery and "to remember what cannot be replaced" (p. 188).

Is cyberspace a First World Netscape that is made on the backs of those who live in Third and Fourth World landscapes?

not just the backs

Joseph Gabilondo (1995) writes that not only does the postmodern, fetishist obsession with the reproduction and simulation of cyborgs replace First World "Man," but cyberspace is a handmaiden to global capitalism. "Capitalism does not get rid of its old technologies and apparatuses; instead it exports them to the Third World" (p. 423). This is evident not only with the creation of free trade zones, export processing zones, and maquiladoras around the world, but also the dumping of toxic waste in economically poorer countries, as well as on the lands of Aboriginal peoples in industrialized countries. There is no such thing as a "postcolonial cyborg" because the cyborg is a hegemonic and privileged subject position of late capitalism, while 'post'colonial subject positions are left outside of cyberspace.

> Postcolonial subject positions are necessary in order to create the outsideness that cyberspace and consumer culture need to constitute themselves as the new hegemonic inner spaces of postmodernism. To put it bluntly, Africa owns 1% of all television sets in the world. (p. 434)

Gabilondo contends that when Haraway wrote her *Manifesto for Cyborgs* in 1985, cyberspace was not as developed as it is today so there was "space for a utopian call." He suggests that the global culture in which we live today cannot be represented or thought out as a presence or agency because the global condition does not exist; "that moment has passed" and it is necessary to "conceptualize and map in order to access it and use it, not utopically but historically" (p. 431).

> *seems to me raven   there's no post anyway when it comes to colonization nobody's gone home*
>
> *well coyote   maybe they forgot the way*
>
> *blackbirds must have eaten the breadcrumbs*

For Derek Gregory (1993), cyborg geographies do not take into consideration the differently constituted places around the integrated circuit:

> For all the appeals to Spivak, Trinh Minh-ha and others, is the cyborg myth a First World fantasy? The electronic and biotechnological freedoms that Haraway anticipates are withheld from many people in many places, and the high technology that she invokes in her deconstruction is disproportionately concentrated in the North/First World. Haraway knows all this of course. (p. 165)

Haraway (1991a) realizes that her cyborg needs redefining in an interview with Constance Penley and Andrew Ross and searches for a "family of displaced figures, of which the cyborg is one" (p. 13), as well as "trickster figures that might turn a stacked deck into a potent set of wild cards for refiguring possible worlds" (p. 24). Haraway cautions of transformation emanating from the practices of the holistic, transcendentalist movements such as New Age because she believes that their alternatives are still in love with technoscience.

Chela Sandoval (1995) looks at a dimension that is left out of much cyborgology, "namely, that cyborg consciousness can be understood as the technological embodiment of a particular and specific form of oppositional consciousness...U.S. third world feminism" (p. 408). She is referring to the "worker who flips burgers, who speaks the cyborg speech of McDonalds"—the cyborg workers of the now dominant global world order. She continues: "My argument has been that colonized peoples of the Americas have already developed the cyborg skills for survival under techno-human conditions as a requisite for survival under domination over the last three hundred years." Sandoval argues for a cyborg methodology for resistance and survival of First World transnational technocultural conditions, "oppositional technologies of power" (p. 409). Her U.S.A. Third World feminism "differential consciousness" technologies have five vectors: semiotic, outsider/within deconstructive, strategic essentialism meta-ideologizing, womanism/moral, and mestiza/world traveling/loving cross-cultures differential.

Both Haraway and Sandoval are writing of a type of joint kinship, lines of affinity, border crossings. Haraway (1991c) writes of "elaborate specificity" and an opportunity for "the loving care people might take to learn how to see faithfully from another point of view" (p. 190).

> *what about power differentials and privilege and getting in the way and taking up all the geography so not knowing how to get out of the way because the only way is your way?*

Can anyone see from another's point of view? Having the "choice" to cross borders and to be in the margins is a privileged and arrogant position. Our seeing can only be partial. If we are not of that land/culture, we do not know the language of the people and of that land. Going to mutindi ndunda's village will not teach me to see from the point of view of the woman who wanted to burn down the coffee crops, or mutindi's mother, or mutindi. I can only see from my body, my understandings and experiences. Looking to the margins, across the borders, and around the world from a western standpoint can easily become another form of imperialism, colonization, and intellectual/academic racism veiled in emancipatory, postmodern, and postcolonial rhetoric. Perhaps caring academics might learn to stand aside so that there is room for those who are less privileged, both at home and around the world, to speak and write for themselves.

> *raven   can you imagine the uproar in the academy   if men spoke for women   if christians spoke for jews   if arabs spoke for buddhists   if straight people spoke for lesbians and gays   how is it still open season on aboriginal peoples?*

> it's simple coyote   it's called tenure and promotion   but what will those
> indian experts do then if they have no one to speak for   instead of?

In later work, Haraway (1997) introduces her new family of displaced figures, a mutated bio-textual-techno figuration that both inhabits and is inhabited by technoscience. Modest_Witness is an e-compression, a spliced hybrid map of knowledge, power, and language—E-Mail, FemaleMan and OncoMouse. Modest_Witness is a diffractive cyborg writing producing "promising interference patterns" (p. 75), an imaginative figuration not only for women but for anyone concerned with the humanist concept of technology as an extension of male freedom, now further extended through global corporate capitalism. Modest_Witness' validity depends on "nurturing and acknowledging alliances with a lively array of others, who are like and unlike, human and not, inside and outside hegemonic selves and powerful places" (p. 269).

Might the popular cultural prodigy of cyborg be another form of orthodoxy and colonization, a new hegemony, a "hybrid global soup" (Rengifo, 1998) in which all difference disappears? For example, Haraway merges cyborg and trickster/Coyote into "trickster cyborgs" (1991b), "cyborgtricksters," and "cyborg-coyotes" (1995). Frédérique Apffel-Marglin (1998) cautions that hybrids are interbreeding and genetic manipulations that make visible the disparate origins of various traits, while rendering invisible tens of thousands of years of the knowledge, work, and inventiveness of the Indigenous peoples who nurtured the varieties of seeds. She argues for a "flowering of diversity—diversity nurtured and strengthened by intercultural cross-pollination" (p. 13). The modesty of Modest_Witness will be demonstrated by who and what constitutes the lively array of others, and how they do, and do not, have access to the New World Order, Inc.—if they so desire.

Tricksteria Pre/re/figures Cyborgia

Within Haraway's (1991c) cyborgian imagery "nature emerges from this exercise as 'coyote,'" a "potent trickster," and "concept of agency" that "can help *us* refigure the kinds of persons we might be" (p. 21, emphasis added).

Virtual(ly) Ed Tech

> *I've been very patient but all this cyborg talk is making me lose my appetite besides I don't remember ever being a trickster in western cultures I've always been the subject of shotgun blasts traps dog attacks and poison bait seems to me there's been some serious cultural appropriation must be some tricksters in white culture? they've been around for a while*

In the same conversation, Haraway suggests that "the subjects are cyborgs, nature is coyote, and the geography is elsewhere" (p. 4).

> *this is the last straw [and the short one] it hurts my back I need to shapeshift this discussion and create a few power outages in the cyborg circuitry and dr frankenstein's in order to bring in some cultural dimensionality so what about this the subjects are characters we are all coyote and donna haraway is elsewhere how can subjects nature and geography be different from one another? only in human language*

Haraway has done much to "provoke rethinking social relationality within artefactual nature" (1991a, p. 23). However, I am concerned about looking to other, to "mestizaje" and "women of color" for help (Haraway, 1992). Gregory (1993) raises questions about another borrowing by Haraway, in particular, "inappropriate/d" from Trinh Minh-ha. Haraway (1992) makes use of "inappropriate/d" as a tactic "not to fit into the *taxon*, to be dislocated from the available maps specifying kinds of actors and kinds of narratives, not to be originally fixed by difference" (p. 299). Minh-ha (1989) uses "inappropriate/d" quite differently, as refusal to know one's "assigned" place, a strategy typically unknown and marginalized in dominant societies.

Haraway calls upon the trickster/Coyote to act as "witty agent" and a "useful myth" to enrich "feminist theory as a reinvented coyote discourse" (1991c, p. 199). Referring to trickster/Coyote, and any narratives of Aboriginal Peoples as "myth" is seen by Peter Cole (2000a) and other Aboriginal scholars as denigrating Aboriginal epistemologies and spiritualities, paving the way for appropriation by the dominant culture.

> *coyotes don't like it too much either*

> *wrrackk us too*

Haraway's understanding of Coyote can only be through her own "situated knowing," to quote Haraway herself. Her understandings of Coyote are informational, whereas Aboriginal Peoples' are relational. Coyote is the will to survival of the human spirit, whereas "coding trickster" cyborgs need to live through, as, and within the codes of information technologies. Theirs is a will to and through technology, a "will to virtuality" (Kroker & Weinstein, 1994). Haraway (1992) writes that the trickster/Coyote has nothing to do with the biological one. Is Haraway referring to a virtual coyote? Can cyborgs be other than hardwired into the technocapitalist machinery? Can Haraway's trickster/Coyote ever become unplugged? Can Coyote become unplugged, both/ and, as well as anything else imagination requires? Can cyborgs become Coyotes? Can anything?

how can haraway understand me when I don't even understand myselves?

Wayne Grady (1994) writes of the tenacity and spirit of coyotes in their struggle to survive (in)humanity, and asks if there can be a border between the coyote howl and the human voice?

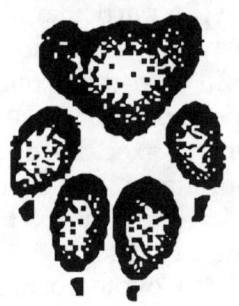

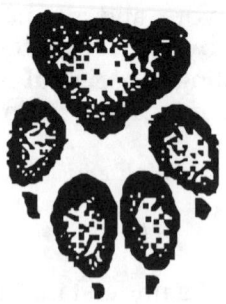

> I listened for nearly half an hour, caught by the haunting melody, fascinated by what was obviously not just a random series of howls but parts of a conversation. The sounds seemed to tremble on the verge of language, to be, almost literally, the voice of wilderness. (p. 13)

Coyote cannot be separated from, and is not other than, the biological coyote and other spirits/actors/subjects, nature, geography, you, and me. The elusive small 'c' coyote continues to outsmart all human endeavour at extermination. Coyotes are survivors despite the tens of millions of government, military, and private dollars and western technologies (steel-jawed traps, poisons, hunting from land and air, burning their dens). Their population and geography keep increasing. Bright (1993) cautions that if we think we can grasp, stabilize, or taxonomize Coyote or try to take over the role of Coyote we will be out-tricked. If we ever think that we have or understand 'it,' Coyote will respond with, "That's not it, that's not it....There was coyote, and there was nothing" (Vizenor, 1994, p. 173).

Coyote keeps dancing through my computer screen, wanting me to play with her but I need to prepare for tomorrow's long journey. Donna, Suzanne, and Noel disappear into the screen as I shut down my computer. There are no goodbyes because we will meet again at the click of a mouse. I shove my laptop, some vitamins, bottled water, a power bar, *Getting Smart*, *Curriculum Visions*, the *The Importance of Being Earnest*, a CD of John Cage's 4'33", and a map of New Jersey into my backpack. I notice that the broken lace in one of my hiking boots I left outside my tent today has been replaced. Coyote turns to the wind and the *aurora borealis* shimmers in the sky behind the snow-covered mountain peaks. Raven, fluffed feathers fluttering, sighs.

A Dataplay

I would rather be a character than a citation.
—Noel Gough, *personal communication*

I love acting. It is so much more real than life.
—Oscar Wilde, *The Picture of Dorian Gray*

Actors come in many and wonderful forms.
Accounts of a 'real' world do not, then, depend on a
logic of 'discovery,' but on a power-charged
social relation of conversation.
—Donna Haraway, *Simians, Cyborgs, and Women*

A light wind is blowing the oak leaves, the bare trees allowing for glimpses of the New York skyline. It is winter, 1998, North Central New Jersey. The sun is setting. I make my way up the marble stairs of a turn-of-the-century brick building on this former estate, now turned into a university. Educational technology graduate students are sitting in a windowless classroom filled with computers. The course is on curriculum inquiry, in particular, en/acting different ways of *re*-generating "data" for educational technology. All of the students are female. Six weeks earlier, after a discussion about different possibilities for writing up "data," I asked if any of them would be interested in being in my data while they are doing their own data. Six volunteered to allow me to take excerpts from their journal writing for the class and to incorporate them into a *dataplay*. I returned a script to them two weeks later for their rewriting. The rest of the students enjoyed this dress rehearsal and decided to join in co-scripting their parts into the play, some drawing on their own data stories. Our *dataplay* is a political act of affirming life, by moving rhizomatically to break with our learned *techno*thinking *techno*subjectivities and reconstituting ourselves as nomadic thinkers and nomadic subjectivities. We become *geoanalysts*, enacting "turbulent unpredictability" (Cage, 1994) in our efforts to remap a different terrain of technology discourses in schools in/and all sorts of whether and weather. Data-ta-ta! ta TA!

Ludic Encounters

Cast of Characters:
    John Cage
    Bill Clinton
    Costume crew
    Coyote (aka Peter Cole)
    Cyborg
    Educational technology graduate students:
        Ainsley
        Amber
        Chris
        Evelyn
        Jessica
        Julia
        Danielle
        Kym
        Lee
        Lori
        Lorraine
        Mary-Lou
    Noel Gough
    Donna Haraway
    Ironed man
    Patti Lather
    Narrator
    Nomad
    Pat O'Riley
    Props crew
    Rhizome
    Elizabeth St Pierre
    Simulac/rum
    James Scheurich
    Stage Manager/Professor
    S-s-stutterer
    Voice-over

Notes to the director:
The truth you are about to portray is fictional.

Notes to the actor:
The fiction you are about to portray is true.

A Dataplay

Notes to the crew:
Ignore the directions of the director and the actions of the actors and use your own common sense and your intuition.

Notes to the front of house:
Speak with the customers nicely—they pay y/our salary.

Notes to the audience/reader:
Grab a rhizome and join in.

General notes:
Please feel free as a reader or audience member to insert your comments. For that purpose, we leave large spaces in the text, the dialogue, the blocking, the play.

Time and place:
Between September 1994 and June 1998, between Vancouver, BC; Melbourne, Australia; Columbus, OH; Wayne, NJ, Warwick, NY; Palmerston North, NZ; Belleville, ON; here, there, every/w/here, nowhere, on and off the reserve.

SFX: (Sharp soprano sax note then a riff)

Enter Narrator in special spot.

SFX: (Beethoven's Fifth)

Narrator: Let the dance begin. Da ta ta ta. Da ta.

Lights out briefly then on again with flashing lights, rotating mirror globe. Whole cast and crew on stage together in freeze frame then dancing to music which suddenly stops. Lights out. Enter Coyote. Dancers are in freeze frame. Spotlight opens on Coyote. Music from Yothu Yindi, Robbie Robertson or Kashtin. Music gradually quietens, and the dancers move offstage and some into freeze frame.

Coyote: *(winks)* I know this dance...but you got to close your eyes when you do it or nothing will happen. You got to close your eyes tight. (King, 1993, p. 77)

Narrator: *(aside)* But, Coyote, she doesn't close her eyes, and all of them start dancing. (King, 1993, p. 77)

Voice-over: You too coyote! Close them.

Coyote: hey   that sounds like raven   hey they didn't put you on the cast list   welcome

Raven: coyote you should know better than to let them put your name on a list   and don't let them put periods after your words   then you're really stuck

Coyote: oh no   not this one   I got punctuation art/illery   and erasure gismos   greetings all   they call me the trickster   my taxonomy card says *canis latrans* but I go by coyote   in different cultures I come in different morphs but for now let's just stick with coyote   this is a story about human beings and language and how they got that way   no solutions are offered or pre/sumed   it'll probably end up being just a bunch of talk and not much listening if it's like the other runs   a lot like everyday life   everybody knows everything and nobody knows the value of not knowing anything except maybe john cage   ah ah ah ah   that's how a coyote laughs because most of the time I'm going backwards in time trying to fix things up that got mussed by people inventing past tenses this is a sight gag so it usually goes over everybody's head except the reader's this play is about rehearsal and collaboration and spontaneity it is about improvisation   it is a script wanting liberation from the page

Lights out, then spots open onto another part of stage. Coyote and a Cyborg are in one spot each: Coyote walks over and puts in big wind-up key into the back of Cyborg. And then a big battery into the Cyborg's costume. Cyborg creaks to life, syllable by syllable.

Cyborg: *SFX: (creak, groan)* Trans/it/ory   trans/it/ive   trans/ition/mission/portation/uranic   trans/world enterprises welcomes you home to the cyberspace of the global village. Well come on in. Trans/it/ory trans/it/ive/   trans/ition/mission...

Coyote makes face and pushes remote to shut Cyborg off.

Coyote: not much of a vocabulary that one   no small talk   no imagination

Enter Ironed Man and Rhizome. Rhizome has many tendrils as befits a rhizome. Coyote gestures with thumb to them. Winks.

Ironed Man: Hi folks! Ironed man, here. Irony is my game. Ferric humour. Ferrous/ed one of all. Ha!

Rhizome: irony *(pause)* is the overproduction of ferric acid   ferrous sulphate culture fair/ic   the neo-cortex makes you not say what you mean to   say what you don't mean to   under/mines your language strip/mines/field   notes with or without   to/from/about   under/ground school   under/education   ground/under school   danger danger

Cyborg turns itself back on with remote control.

Cyborg: *SFX: (creak)* Delve into the monster's belly. Let it colon/ize you, ingest you. Delve down.

Voice-over: Ground yourself. Any/every/thing if you want to finetune in to your station of choice, get aerial borne again.

Coyote: but attend ground school first   under ground   test your theories first on a simulator unless you trust your wings your aero/dynamics.

SFX: (Coyote howls)

Rhizome: don't sub/ob/ject/ify/igate yourself   your talk   control the nomads   the sub/text/terranian/trusive/marine   sandwiches

Enter Nomad who roams about the stage and enters and exits at will during the whole play, acting and speaking improvisationally. Nomad is dressed for all kinds of weather/whether.

Cyborg: *(moves stiffly)* Pre/position   lo/cate   lo/calize   lo/cativize parse everything how do you parse what's not there   case your talk person it get across your point   your point across your line across your geo/metric   across via/ducts   obscure bridges going nowhere joining nothing   nobody knows about "about"   if they understand what you're about they'll take you down with the weapons of language how do you say herecomethelanguage police in a code they can't trans/iter/ oops/tool/ate.

SFX: (Coyote howls)

Voice-over: I am the voice of else/where, other/wise, knowing without knowing using avalanches groundswells of words to re/miss/perimutuel/circumspect/direct/ionalize.

Enter Stutterer; Coyote blows bubbles around stage—dances.

Stutterer: Ll l l let gggggo of know   and other   /iiiings   l l l let loose of rather than wwwith words. *(begins to sing)* K k k katie b beautiful Katie, y you're the only g g g girl that I adore. Wh when the m m moon shines over the c cowshed, I'll be w waiting at the k k k kitchen door. *(begins to sing in sign—American Sign Language)*

Ironed Man: W what's wrong C cy? You look d down.

Cyborg: It's about the industrial revolution. It didn't l last l long enough. I was born too late to participate.

Voice-over: Too late? I thought it was still going on. Could you be more specific?

Cyborg: No. I can't be. I am a global general sort of person. I do not deal with specifics, specifications, specificities. I have no time left once I'm done with the generals. And field marshals, not to mention their horses and all the e-MAI/l, WTO, NAFTA, FTAA.

Voice-over: Spare us the latter translation.

Cyborg: Please do not erase.

Pat O'Riley: Gilles Deleuze says humour is fourth person singular.

Coyote: so that's why the english language never had a sense of humour   and if you can't be funny in fours you can always start a quartet

Enter Professor with mortar (and pestle) and convocation robes. Professor is also Stage Manager, just with a different mask. Sits.

SFX: (musical riff)

Voice-over: Ahem. I have been told there is a learnéd self *ipse dixit (pause)* professor hereabouts. An esteemed person of much *(ahem)* learning.

Professor: Do you have an appointment? I'm busy until the year 2009.

Voice-over: You are popular. Well it just so happens I rang up your secretary and he...

Professor: Said what? That we have a cancellation and he'd pencil you in? I don't recall an invisible person in my appointment book. Name?

Voice-over: I am else/where and other/wise. You've been raking the ground a lot lately on the subject of validity. Maybe try summerfallow. It's an alter/native means of sustainable semio/en/ culturation.

Professor: Can you get to a point? We have theatre to per/form. Off-the-street persons are not welcome to attend rehearsals.

Voice-over: You've been proclaiming yourself an expert on data analysis 'round town.

A Dataplay

SFX: *(theme of Beethoven's Fifth)*

Iron Man: Da ta ta ta DA ta dadadadadada TA.

Stage Manager: *(removes mask)* Look, mister or ms or what/whoever you are, buy a ticket for the show. We have work to do and you were not invited. I did not call a press conference. Don't muss with our rehearsal time.

Voice-over: I don't see any act/ors. I just see a bored audience hohumming.

Stage Manager: Where?

SFX: *(Raven's wraaak)*

Voice-over: Just off the page where the dialogue is printed, where the words are per/formed. Your thoughts on research methodology have been whirla-gigging like lost birds.

Professor: *(mask on)* You have places to go. Pressing engagements. Cheerio. Adieu. Goodbye. Farewell. Ciao.

Coyote: she got airmiles   kilometres in canada

Professor: *(looking toward soundbooth)* If you have a point, spew. I have a life. You must have better things to do than sit in the sound booth with terminal lallorhea. Chuckle away you twit. Wipe that grin off your beak.

Coyote: beak?   there is no-one in the sound booth professor   she's in the air like ariel   hello   wake up   smell the muzak

Voice-over: Profess *(pause)* or, you think too much with your head.

Professor: What do you think with?

Voice-over: I don't have *(pause)* to. I have ten *(pause)* ure.

Professor: For an unbibliographized, uncontexted, discursive nonperson, you do a lot of interrupting.

Voice-over: It's my role. I've insinuated myself into your play.

Professor: You're not in the script.

Voice-over: I am extracursive. Impromptu. Improvisational.

Professor: For heaven's sake. Have your say and be gone. Where did you say you did your graduate work—BSU?

SFX: *(Coyote howls)*

Cyborg: SFX: *(croaky, coming to life)* Don't know about the voice. I don't know that I like this voice you gave me. I want a different voice. I did my graduate work in the lab/or/a/tory. I was labbed. I was oratoried. I did graduate work nowhere and everywhere. Bits and bytes at Global U. RAM DAM A DOO DOO Humpty Dumpty pixel mixel patta patta fixel.

Professor: You wouldn't be pretending to be André Breton, Lao Tzu, Carol Burnett, Gilles Deleuze lapsing paraffin with banal profundities?

Voice-over: I don't have a catching glove for that kind of humour.

Coyote: pitching arm not too good either   whirlagag a doo

SFX: *(Coyote howls)*

Voice-over: I want to talk about validity.

Stage Manager: Look you, we've got a play to practice up for.

Coyote: *(clicks remote, freezing Professor)* or is it a practice to play up for?

Ironed Man: Hooooo! Ending a sentence in not one but two pre/positions. Next you'll be conjuncting all over the place, splitting infinitives.

Coyote: that's not in the script stayprest   and I'll do the humour   ing around here

SFX: *(Coyote howls)*

Cyborg: Who gave you the author/ity to run things?

Coyote: who's askin' wind-up?

Cyborg shuts down. Professor exits. Lights out, then up on an educational technology graduate seminar. Pat O'Riley is reading A Columbus Coyote Story by Thomas King to twelve graduate students sitting in a big circle. Patti Lather is sitting crosslegged on top of the desk at the front of the room in conversation with Noel Gough, Elizabeth St. Pierre, and James Scheurich. John Cage is sitting at a piano, Donna Haraway at a computer.

SFX: *(John Cage plays his silent piece, 4'33" on a miniature piano.)*

John Cage: *(stops playing, begins blowing soap bubbles which Coyote tries to bite)* "Sound is merely bubbles on the surface of silence" (1961, p. 32).

Coyote: bubbles contain the noise of silence   people hate   silence   it's like a mirror mirror on the wall   it offends them which is to say they are offended by   it *(howls)*   me too   I like sounds especially my own *(sings)* you ain't nothin' but an old coy o te   howlin' all the time ain't never caught a bad habit and you ain't no friend of...

Pat O'Riley: *(interrupting Coyote)* Let's start today by talking about how it is that computers have been given such a prominent place in the classroom; however, there has been little research or critical dialogue in education to support the huge amount of monies spent on computers.

Coyote: ask david noble   have a fireside chat with noam chomsky   you got the threads between your neck and your head all stripped   either go metric or imperial/ist   and don't complain to me   if you got stuck on a picket fence

Cyborg: Get into the modern world. Put some money down on a semi-detached wired bungalow. Live for today for tomorrow is...

Voice-over: *(singing)* Promised to no-one...

SFX: *(Raven's wrraaaaack)*

Coyote: hey   you all   do it   start payments on a new gasguzzler sportsutility vehicle   got to have a four-wheel drive to go to the grocery store   potato chips coke and fluffy cookies are hard on the suspension   next year they'll all be driving eight-wheel drive 10-ton triple axle hummers to pick up the kids some mctreats   good for the environment   all that gas mm   smells like newark chardonnay 1983   maybe eau de lodi   got to DRIVE the kids to school   they can't walk

Cyborg: Get uptodate. Leave the past behind in the dust. Modernize.

Coyote: I'm a dipsy doodle dandy   come one come all to the new age of information   bring your scoop shovels and your thimbles and your melmac cups   get your paw out of that pie   that's right folks   step right up and commodificate before it's too late   buy buy   mercenaries for sale or rent

Simulac/rum: *(reflecting off Cyborg)* On the other hand why not just pull out your plastic money   charge up a trip for the whole family to Disneyland or Las Vegas or better yet buy the latest computer war games—virtual violence virtual destruction virtual elimination. Welcome to the West.

Voice-over: Just leave your firearms with the sheriff.

SFX: *(howls)*

Coyote: I've got videogames I got video   I got videogames enough to last me all my life   at least until the next generation comes up

SFX: *(Beach Boys' Let's Surf) (Coyote surfs on large mousepad)*

Cyborg: Plug in. Turn power switch on. Adjust vertical control. Insert disk. Do not question. Inter/net.

Danielle: Our students are being so influenced by the technological world around them that they claim to be easily "bored," and can hardly stay in their seats long enough to attend to what you are teaching. We constantly feel as though we are competing with the computers, the video games, the MTV world, and other outside stimuli.

Coyote: outside?   I thought they were inside

Noel Gough: *(interrupting Coyote)* "While...many of us live inside enormous novels...our subjectivities—and certainly those of many young people—also reside (at least partially) in enormous videos, movies, computer games, and body languages" (1995, p. 73).

Coyote: *SFX: (sings)* what good is sitting all alone in your room   come watch el niño play

Cyborg: Stay in your room. Go into that computing place. Zero in. Get screened. Virtualize. Plug in. Plug in. Plug in. Plug in.

Coyote: computers are no good for coyotes   the keys are too close together and we have no thumbs for the spacebar and the screen doesn't take into account the length of our noses   they get in the way of looking   besides there's nothing to eat in cyberspace   there's not even room to run around   or turn around

Lorraine: The great thing about computers is the fact that they can allow children to have pen pals all over the world without having to wait for the postman to deliver the letter. Email is instant and worldwide. The Internet is an incredible source of information, not all of it accurate or worthy of being on the net, but nevertheless it is an awesome tool to teach children about other cultures. You can experience the world—virtually and interact with it, to an extent, via the Internet and telecommunications. People are able to access all kinds of information at the press of a button, which has unlocked a whole new world of knowledge. You can now search the web for ethnic recipes if you'd like and you would probably find just about everything you were looking for and a whole lot more.

Simulac/rum: Don't need knowledge, just information. Don't need real, just virtual.

Coyote presses remote control and turns on the television stage left.

Bill Clinton: "The new promise of the global economy, the Information Age, unimagined new work, life-enhancing technology—all these are ours to seize" (1997).

Coyote: he means steal or murder to get them

Bill Clinton: "We must bring the power of the Information Age into all our schools. Last year, I challenged America to connect every classroom and every library to the Internet by the year 2000, so that, for the first time in our history, children in the most isolated rural town, the most comfortable suburbs, the poorest inner city schools, will have the same access to the same universe of knowledge" (1996).

Cyborg: It does not com pute. Domain error. Error of type -23.

Coyote makes a face and turns the television off, joins the seminar circle.

Elizabeth St. Pierre: "If we entertain the possibility that all might not be what we have been led to believe—that there might be worlds other than the one described by liberal humanism, then poststructural theories offer opportunities to investigate those worlds by opening up language for deployment in revitalized social agendas" (1997, p. 176).

Kym: We are much like the children we teach each day:
Questioning
Searching for answers
Love of learning
Longing for knowledge
Seeking guidance into a whole new world
Unfamiliar in many ways
Slightly scared of the unknown
Comforted by answers from a trusted
Hero or Shero, an educator

Pat O'Riley: Novel approach, Kym.

Coyote: poetic approach   kym

Cyborg: Well come on in to the new industrial revolution. Free silicon chips for every body. Just bring your own dip.

Coyote: *(sings)* stuff stuff stuff stuff   stuff stuff stuff stuff   stuff stuff stuff stuff "We don't need that stuff. You got to stop making all those things. You're going to fill up this world" (King, 1993, p. 76).

John Cage: "Our intention is to affirm this life, not to bring order out of chaos, nor to suggest improvements in creation, but simply to wake up to the very life we living which is so excellent when we put our desires out of its way and let it act of its own accord" (1961, p. 12).

Cyborg: *(interrupting John Cage)* New hardware all around. New everything. Snap out the old snap in the new. Snap out the knew; snap in the know.

Simulac/rum: Don't question. Just produce, process, reproduce, reprocess. Buy buy.

Chris: Technology is the future, there is no doubt, but it's a future *with* technology not a future designed around technology.

Kym: Sure technology is the way of the future but you need to look for the "happy medium." Yes, we know how to use technology, but do we know when, or if it is right for our children?

Elizabeth St. Pierre: "We must learn to live in the middle of things, in the tension of conflict and confusion and possibility; and we must become adept at making do with the messiness of that condition and at finding agency with rather than assuming it in advance of the ambiguity of language and cultural practice" (1997, p. 176).

Pat O'Riley: Does technology affect teachers' jobs?

Lorraine: Sometimes I wonder if teachers are frightened they will be replaced/lose their jobs. I do not feel that the increase in technology poses any threat to jobs. However I do believe that some people may/will be displaced. There will be an increase in jobs but there will be a different kind of job and therefore more/different training will be required. I believe we will see a further decrease in manufacturing jobs and yet an increase in demand for workers in the service sectors. Those who do manufacture computers must be protected—working conditions/health issues must be addressed.

Pat O'Riley: What about sharing jobs, living differently, doing with less?

Cyborg: Do not share jobs. Jobs are for machines. I love work. It makes me strong. It makes me feel good. I love to work over/time. It makes me lots of money I can use to buy more things.

Coyote sits on the edge of a desk, puts glasses on her nose, dangles her feet, and leafs through "A Coyote Columbus Story."

Coyote: I loooove this book   it doesn't mean anything to me   but it's my favourite

Patti Lather: "Reading without understanding is required if we are to go beyond the imaginary 'real' of history" (1996, p. 528).

Simulac/rum: I like to discover new maps. I am not interested in territory because it changes. Maps are my specialty. I jump right in and get lost and never worry about anybody else's reality. Code uncode.

Kym: I enjoyed listening to *A Coyote Columbus Story*. I thought it had a unique spin to it. I think the way in which it was presented really allowed the reader, in our case, the listener, to make his/her own inferences on the way the world is. It did not conform us to a view of the way things are; rather it gave us the chance to question what we might have always wanted to question but were told "that's the way it is."

Elizabeth St. Pierre: "We are in play, working on the verge of intelligibility with no guarantee of liberation" (1997, p. 176). "To play in the possibilities of that space outside language that is opened when words fall apart is my desire" (p. 186).

Coyote: I tried the outside of language   but there were too many words trying to get in   and the silence   oh   the silence   it made me howl *(howls)* give me language   give me words   give me a preposition or two   give me lots of verbs and nouns and inbetween and while you're at it make me a quick cappuccino *(howls)*

Cyborg: I don't need anything except money and memory chips. I don't need to know anything—I have RAM and harddrive. Glip. Glip. Put away those books and get out your laptops.

Coyote: I don't have a lap

Cyborg: Then sit down!

Coyote: I enjoyed being read readed   rode   e rode de/ride   but I got a bit sad dle sore   we coyote's weren't aren't built for horsetravel gid dee yap

Lorraine: We must take into account cultural differences and must strive to find the benefits of each perspective. Makes me think of *Babe*, the movie, the animals lived and behaved based on stereotypes and they had one another. The sheep hated the dogs and call them wolves and the dogs thought the sheep were stupid and the cat said the pigs' only purpose was bacon. The brown chickens only stayed with the brown chickens and the whites with the white ones. Then along comes Babe—he is innocent and unbiased, or so it seems, and sees the good in everyone—should we try to be like Babe?

Coyote: hey! what about me!   those who call themselves the first worlds think of me as third world and I live right here   I have lots of technology   those first worlds just can't see it   they have screens   I have scents *(sniffs)*

Pat O'Riley: Have you thought any more about gender and technology since our class discussion two weeks ago?

Evelyn: I never gave much thought to gender equity before. My feelings regarding technology, gender, and culture are changing how I am teaching technology in my classroom.

Lee: I have begun to notice gender issues in technology more frequently. I honestly didn't notice them too much before. Because of the topics we have discussed in class, I am considering doing my thesis on something related to gender.

Lorraine: How much technology in urban areas is dedicated to drill and practice? I do notice that the girls like the word processing/composing/cut and paste parts of the classes and the boys like the straight copying/accounting/graphics; I encourage them to try both.

Cyborg: Hup two three four/about/march/present arms. Men always remember you are soldiers first.

Lorraine: Computers ignore the sense of smell and touch and taste—they are, at least for now, purely visual and auditory stimulation which only gives you a piece of the picture. You are limited by the interpretation of the person who put together the program or filmed the video footage you scroll through. I wonder what aspects of the tree were left out or went unnoticed when the program or video was made? How can we say that by presenting matter in one form, by one view, that we are letting our children fully experience all that we are teaching them? We should let them go out and touch the bark and leaves, play in the shade, climb on the branches—fully experience the tree and bring to it all of their knowings and past experiences. They may discover something we otherwise would have never thought of. Only by experiencing all different senses can we truly connect. The computer is still a virtual world.

Evelyn: I am concerned with the "docile bodies" we are creating with the use of technology. Children need to play with and converse with each other in order to get along socially. They need to witness body language, hear different verbal expressions and dialects and converse in person to remain human.

Lee: One of the faculty members in my school is afraid that the students are going to lose fine motor skills that we develop by practicing handwriting. He feels that all of the typing we do will hurt children's motor skills and eventually have tremendous negative effects on the use of our thumbs.

Evelyn: Some of the children have parents who even pick up lunch for them at McDonald's and drive it to them at school. Walking or riding bikes is almost a lost art. This lack of exercise is also becoming more and more apparent on their little bodies.

Donna Haraway: "Our machines are disturbingly lively, and we ourselves are frighteningly inert" (1991c, p. 152).

Coyote: I think I'm surprisingly ert   considering my age   and what I've been through

Lee: Is faster and easier always better? Are we just getting lazy? I see a large number of overweight students in the elementary grades of my school. Is technology taking away the physical activity that we performed in our youth? Are the fast foods that children are eating full of preservatives and artificial flavorings and colorings that may eventually compromise the health of these generations?

Mary-Lou: I believed that computers developed skills in ways they would never have been otherwise achieved. Ra-Ra mentality—can't get enough —it is a necessity since everyone every job will use a computer. Sharpen those computer skills, they are as important as academia.

Coyote: that's right **SFX:** (*howls*) if you don't spend you could be charged with sedition or high treason   or heresy

Lee: Before taking this course, I would only consider high tech devices. The low tech devices seemed to slip my mind. It is not that I didn't know they existed or that I didn't know that a pen and paper are high tech in some culture, I guess I was only thinking of myself and my culture and my experiences. I do consider pen and paper technology in my culture, it is low tech, but it is still technology. The high tech "newer, faster, better" peripherals are what I would have thought of first. I sometimes get caught up in the hype of the businesses producing these technologies.

Evelyn: I always thought that technology was the way of the future. After reading many articles, I am somewhat skeptical about technology in education. I never thought that I would think this way, but I no longer feel guilty when my students are not spending as much time on the classroom computers. I want to slow down, evaluate my software programs, and use them in a more meaningful manner in my classroom.

Lorraine: If asked what I thought technology was a year ago, I would have answered computers and software. So many people think of technology as limited to computers because ultimately that is what we are bombarded with each day. Technology to me can be so many things —anything that helps you complete a task, no matter how crude it seems—I fell victim to the trap that it had to have all of the whistles and bells if it was to be considered technology—how could they consider a book technology—it cannot move or solve an equation or retrieve information. It can, however, supply valuable information, show you how to solve an equation. Granted it must be in steps and you must manually manoeuver through them.

Lee: (*writing with a pen on overhead—writing increases in size with each sentence*) Low tech/hi tech both have dis/advantages; however, today I un/dis/covered one very big disadvantage of hi tech and one extremely big advantage of low tech (computer vs my pen). Computer (writing) cannot express my emotions as clearly as pen or one's own handwriting. Several hours have passed since writing journal entries. Look again over the beginning, continue looking over each page toward the end. No one can deny the emotion/expression of the writer!

Lorraine: David Noble is right that technology, or the use of it, is not top on every teacher's list. We struggle with kids' social/family/drug/peer problems. We struggle to teach our kids how to live. Tech represents an escape from these struggles, a bandaid!

Julia: I think about gender, culture, and environment.

Lorraine: I work to integrate environmental awareness into lessons. Recycling has become a hot topic. We discuss workers, conditions. Students have become interested as well; I give them extra credit if they bring in articles from newspapers, magazines regarding environment. I require my students to THINK—think about this/that. I tell them they can make a difference. Just as adults are responsible for youngsters now, I remind them that they will someday be responsible for me and the world I live in. The circle of life continues!

Evelyn: Environment is an issue that I feel needs to be taught to all children. Since we are such a throw-away society, it is important to teach children how to recycle. We also need to be thinking about where we will be dumping our waste. Pollution is a large concern.

Lorraine: Talked to my kids about environmental issues (since they brought up great weather we are having!). Hey it's January and this is NJ—don't you wonder why we have no snow? Did you read about the colossal icebergs breaking up in Antarctica? Don't throw away batteries and buy new ones instead purchase rechargeable ones! We have become a disposable society—don't need to throw it away. No—either do with less or recycle.

Coyote: emission transmission *SFX: (fart)* clean air clean air *(muffles fart in paper bag)* experiment not always duplicable *SFX: (fart)*

Lee: I am a firm believer that most technology is very useful. However it is just a tool. One that can be overused and that can cause damage.

Lorraine: I play around with language. Technology is tightening its rei/g/ns. I use the yesterday/today/tomorrow scenario weekly and sometimes more. I encourage the students to think about their use of language. Do they communicate their thoughts clearly? Is there a difference in student talk and grown-up talk? Do you use both? I let the students know that I too am a student in my classroom. I am not afraid to let them know that I don't know and that I enjoy learning with them.

Mary-Lou: I notice a change in attitude throughout my classroom. The students have taken charge of their own learning. We read a poem, *If I Were to Change the World*, by Judith Vorst. I then asked the students to rewrite the poem as if they were in charge of the world. Their responses were incredible!

Amber: We discussed a technology high school in Napa Valley, California, that preps the students for high tech jobs and involves a curriculum that connects teamwork and computers. The climate of the school is said to be "businesslike." Some of the students are even given vacation days. This type of environment sounds great to me as long as they are also preparing these students for social skills as well as business skills. The jobs that will be out there for these students will be high tech jobs. However, the basics that have always been out there from my grandparents through to my parents, to me and still continuing are the social concepts of respect for others, cooperation and understanding. Teachers are needed to discuss and guide the students on human relationships.

Danielle: I resent the fact that big business is using school budgets in an attempt to bolster its own lagging profits. I resent the fact that big business is making itself look like the Good guy by offering contests, impressive prizes, technical support, etc. when, in the end, it will be the big winner. I resent the fact that CEOs of major technological companies, whether it be computers or telecommunications, are also sitting as chairmen of committees that they can influence and ultimately benefit from. But, perhaps, most of all, I resent the fact that Roger Schank would replace teachers with computers since [according to him] most teachers are intellectually and temperamentally ill equipped to deal with schoolchildren. Will computers be able to temperamentally deal with children? Will they have feelings at all? And if children learn a lot by following role models, what will they turn into?

Cyborg: Technology prepares you to be an efficient cog.

Danielle: Why do we use our children as guinea pigs? I often ask myself this question. Many of the educational practices we so quickly introduce to our children are often-times thrown out after a few years when somehow it is surprisingly discovered that the technique did not work. Take for example whole language. You don't just throw out ideas that have been successful for the sake of innovation. And in some cases, I fear this is what technology without "healthy skepticism" is doing.

Lorraine: Why must we follow? Why don't we initiate? I am insulted by Schank's comments that "most teachers are ill equipped to deal with schoolchildren." It is those in industry who are ill equipped and do not know how to deal with emotions/problems/baggage of children.

Danielle: Or what about the report, just this past week, that New York City is spending thousands of dollars on art work to display in the schools. They passed some suggestion that the schools needed this art. Again it made me think—just as they need technology. The students they interviewed said they needed textbooks and supplies more than they needed these works of art. Is this the same way that some districts are misspending funds on technology?

Coyote: "Some of these stories are flat....That's what happens when you try to fix this world. This world is pretty good all by itself. Best to leave it alone. Stop messing around with it" (King, 1994, p. 80).

SFX: (Coyote howls)

Evelyn: Glad to see the word is getting out about the MAI [Multilateral Agreement on Investment]—a failed global corporate power grab. I have a child of a congressman in my class. I plan to speak to him about the MAI.

SFX: (Beethoven's Fifth theme played by John Cage)

Cyborg: MAIMAIMAI MAIIII MAIII MAIMAIMAI   MAI day   eMAI l *(sings)* MAI be I'm right   and MAI be I'm wrong   doo wacka do multilateral agreement on investment M m Mai m mai m m m mai m mai who put the Mai in the Mai Mai Mai Mai Mai? *(improvising to the tune of other songs)*

Mary-Lou: The tactics being used in the MAI can be paralleled to the arguments and treaties being negotiated in public education. Just as "big business" is running the country, so too is the political agenda in public education

Elizabeth St. Pierre: "Ethics is no longer transcendental and clearly defined in advance for everyone in every situation. Rather, ethics explodes anew in every circumstance, demands a specific reinscription, and hounds praxis unmercifully" (1997, p. 176).

Coyote: hounds   haaa rooooo!

Pat O'Riley: Has the conversation we've had in this technology/research seminar given you any ideas about how you might approach your own research project on computers and education?

Lorraine: I think I am a better, more aware, more thoughtful person. Things I would have never thought about that mattered. I now look for the unseen, the unheard and the unobserved. I want to know what wasn't said—I have begun to look for perspectives other than my own.

Kym: We discussed something that really made me think about the importance of perspective and how much a difference it can make in research and interpretation. The discussion revolved around a map of New Zealand where New Zealand was the central focus on the map. How different this must be than the way we are accustomed to looking at things. That is the whole key—gaining new perspectives.

Lorraine: What relevance does any of this software have to us. Kids clicking on a color palette and coloring on the screen! Use a crayon—learn to hold a crayon and color/shade/outline—learn to write and print the alphabet rather than punch a key on the keyboard. The teachers complain there is not enough time for all they must teach. Quit playing on the computer and you will have plenty more time.

Kym: I am intrigued by andragogy. We not only learn from the professors, but from one another and our own experiences. And the professors learn from us. I can then take this manner of learning and/or teaching and use it in my classroom.

Lorraine: I don't always look at the obvious and try to realize my biases when planning a lesson or anything at all. Be aware of the cultural differences and realize how what you see as fine may highly offend someone of another culture. Also search for gender biases when you preview software or even in the articles that you read. It certainly is not such a big earth. Somehow we are all connected. I have become more aware of global warming/environmental issues. I realize that I can make a difference in their environment, perhaps individually on a small scale. But as a teacher, I realize, I reach 125 students daily and that is a much larger scale!

Jessica: I am more aware of other cultures, especially First Nations cultures. I did not pay much attention to cultural differences in technology. I was the typical self-centered American, too wrapped up in my own world thinking what's good for me should be good for everyone else. I wasn't considering other cultures and what is good for them. I didn't realize that those decisions should be made from within the culture.

Ainsley: As teachers we need to be more critical, we need to take the blinders off. We have an incredible responsibility to these kids. Standardizing curriculum is manufacturing consent.

Pat O'Riley: Some of the lessons we learn can be very difficult for us. Learning to look at the world differently can be painful. It can sometimes leave us feeling powerless.

Evelyn: I could see myself in many different areas of Lather's article, *Staying Dumb? Student resistance in liberatory curriculum*. Many of her students had the same reactions that I am currently experiencing. I am realizing how naïve I am while also questioning what I am learning. A great deal of what I am experiencing in class and reading is very hard for me because I don't want to know that it exists. I guess there is an element of denial here. I am gaining new insight but am questioning myself at the same time. I understand that some of these issues are real, but what can I do about them? How can I make a difference?

Mary-Lou: At first I wondered why the "s" on the end of truth. Now I am beginning to understand that the "s" is the most important part of truth.

Pat O'Riley: How do you feel about being in someone else's 'data' as you write up your own data stories?

Lori: I would like to say how difficult it was for me to write poetic responses. It was not finding the words to the poems that was hard, but really getting in touch with how I felt about the questions you asked.

Julia: When you first explained the play to us, I was not sure how the information would be presented. I like the way the citations are spoken.

Ainsley: I thought the idea of characters was wonderful. Coyote was very funny. I have never been exposed to anything like that before. Data are not just the answer; they are always the question.

Kym: It is amazing to see even your (my) own words take on more meaning [in this play] than I had truly intended for them. It opened up another opportunity for me to learn from you and from myself. Using our voices gave us a chance to speak and be heard. By including us, it has really brought it all to life. Our part in the play really shows how much we have learned individually and together. I have learned a lot, a lot more than I ever expected to learn.

Lee: I always have a picture of the trickster in the back of my mind. That helps me poke fun at myself. The trickster allows me to acknowledge there are many ways to look at things. Sometimes I do not like this. I feel that it makes a shamble of my thoughts and words.

Patti Lather: "It is not a matter of looking harder or more closely, but seeing what frames our seeing—spaces of constructed visibility and incitements to see which constitute power/knowledge" (1993, p. 675).

Coyote: *(Wipes glasses with tail)* these glasses they keep getting smudged   I can't see like I used to

Jessica: At times I would like to be ignorant. It is easier to just believe what you read or observe and not look beneath the surface. That is what I have done up until now. Searching for validity complicates the issues.

James Scheurich: "What is needed is research on interviewing itself—some "playing around" or experimentation with interviewing and with ways to represent interviews that highlight the indeterminacy of interview interactions, ways that allow for the uncontrollable play of power within the interaction" (1995, p. 250).

Mary-Lou: I am thinking of writing my data stories in the form of a conversation. Whenever I engage in conversation with my students, I feel as though they really understand what is going on. If they do not know, they are not afraid to question. I had them critique their own presentations. Their questions were wonderful. We used their questions in our reflections survey. That was much more valid than anything I could have done.

Lee: In previous classes my research always ended in a conclusion. How can a conclusion be reached? No work (research) is ever complete. I like how Lather ended *Staying Dumb* with a quoted poem. We need to look at research in this way. I'm going to continue my data collection by creating a third tale that includes dialogue between my students and myself. *Data as dialogue*. Since they are the reason for my research, they are the subjects I should include. It would give my research more validity.

Coyote: oh boy   it looks like we got to do this all over again

SFX: (Coyote howls)

"Those [researchers] push their tape recorders, fix their cameras. All of those ones smile. Nod their head around. Look out window. Shake my hand. Say happy noises. Say goodbye, see you later. Leave pretty quick. We watch them go. My friend put the pot on for some tea. I clean up all the coyote tracks on the floor" (King, 1993, p. 10).

Joining Landscape and Epistemologies

> New ideas come from the desert, from hermits, from solitary beings, from those who live in retreat and are not plugged into the sound and fury of repetitive discussion. The latter always makes too much noise to enable one to think clearly.
> —Michel Serres & Bruno Latour, *Conversations on Science, Culture, and Time*

> When we shift our gaze from the particular to the interconnected and to the generativity of all life and creation, a sense of awe arises. Such a shift lets us see the order in nature (complex), the symmetry (recursive), and the balance (dynamic).
> —William E. Doll, Jr., *The Journey of Spirit and Democratic Education*

How refreshing it is to wake up to this plateau, away from the madness of high tech. A morning walk, taking time to smell the air, to feel the moss, see the lichen in all their subtle colours, the dew, the early morning sounds of life in celebration. It is here where I feel least like a researcher, least like I want to be involved in this kind of invasive activity. I found this plateau by following signs—blazes—which I think were set up by Coyote or Raven. I followed them without really realizing I was. On this plateau, I am getting away from the words, the wording, engaging more with the land/scape. However, my appreciation for being here comes not just in bodily sensations, and emotional feelings, and spiritual tendrils, but also a putting into language. This is how I have learned to share. Painting and poetry, dance, music—these can all be fairly broad in their appeal, but there is something about language. That should seem obvious because I am using language to say it.

This writing journey has been a call for technology discourses that respect all peoples, all living things, and this planet with "historical lucidity a matter not of clarity but of justice" (Shohat & Stam, 1994, p. 359). This plateau is a "repetition, another layer, the return of the same, a catching on of something else, an imperceptible difference, a coming apart and ineluctable tearing open" (Deleuze, 1995, p. 84) of the previous plateaux in the hope of opening technology discourses in education to different "expressibles" (Deleuze, 1994a). I unfold and refold (*plus de plis*) my maps of this journey to seek isomorphic conjunctions by juxtapositioning or otherwise montaging dialogue, situation, and theory so that different connections and directions might syncretize from (and perhaps despite) the paths I have taken during this writing journey. My hope is that others will join in an effort to deterritorialize, reconstitute, and extend the terrain of technology discourses so that flows are distributed rather than restricted. I work to cocreate *un*disciplinary spaces that perpetually interrogate hierarchy and the formation of corporate education—a move from reiteration of regulatory schema to regeneration, and from a material path to a more spiritual path.

Telling Different Stories

John Willinsky (1998) maintains that the "responsibility of an 'advanced civilization' was assumed to be to make the world fathomable and sensible for the benefit of all humankind" (p. 52). With most of humankind being left behind, what does advanced mean—advanced materially? As mutindi ndunda once said to me when talking about what western imperialism, colonialism, and recent economic development projects have done to her people, their way of life, and their land, "Who are the civilized?" As I write this, I can hear the beating of George Bush's war drum, and the rhetoric about freedom-loving and democracy from a country whose history, like Canada's, is bloodied by the extermination of millions of the original inhabitants of that land—its First Peoples. Rhetoric cannot erase or deny enacted genocides; it can only keep the patina of civility, the storefront of democracy, of f(r)eedom, fresh for a few more units of time. Willinsky proposes supplementing our education with teaching of imperialism's [and neoimperialism's], influence on schooling, in the hope that it will change how this legacy works on us.

Coyote wakes up to the word legacy and backforms the rest of the discussion, based on the seed word.

> is that what they call it   left behind   is that why they all go to their lake cottages on the weekend   is that why "wilderness" trekking is becoming so popular?   so now they want to have courses that will teach us how we're being duped subliminal seduction   level 68   welcome class   let's get right down to the readings   today we're looking at imperialism   from cutaneous to subcutaneous   organic solutions to preventing genocide

To supplement is not to add on, but "to learn again, rather than to imagine walking away from being the educated subjects we have become" (p. 263).

> what do we learn with   what are the contexts   where does all this 'educated' learning get us   how is it that popular education never reaches the coyote poisoners   the rednecks   the kkk?

Learning again will require displacing image and information with a shared and storied engagement in the world, reshaping western patriarchal *techné* into a more poetic *techné as poiesis* and poethics joining body, spirit, and land.

> who's going to do all this shaping?   western educated   brown   yellow   black people   white allies?   will western methods of de-briefing de-propagandizing be used?   will well-meaning ignorant academics just change the shape and scent of prejudice   will they wallpaper over it?   there's always an expert with answers   with the 'right' formula   pat/ent answers   where did those answers come from?   were they hiding under a semantic bush or were they pulled out of the err   pooof!

There needs to be an examination of how our past has become the present which is then displaced into the future, of how western "high" technologies have become foregrounded in education while eclipsing, and occulting Indigenous and other sustainable technologies, of how education has become a training ground for global corporate capitalism, and of how learning has become disconnected from land and spirit. When training takes the place of education, it becomes obvious that the profit-above-all-else lobby has become government, superceded it. There was a story on the CBC

TV 6 o'clock news on September 9, 2002, about organized crime becoming more noticeably active in Canada's ports—smuggling people, alcohol, drugs, weapons. The spokesperson for a national policing organization said that profit was the motive—at any cost. Sound familiar?

Noel Gough (1995) suggests that educators think of any curriculum narrative as a "collective story we tell our children about our past, our present, and our future" (p. 71). He adds that curriculum narratives are not only configured as collective, but selective stories. In the case of technology education, the selection of stories is prescribed "for all students" by a small group of (mostly white male) former industrial educators, allied with (mostly white male) engineers, scientists, and business interests. Gough maintains that realist curriculum stories "largely ignore the ways in which agency is *produced* by and within the complex circuits and relays that connect, contingently reinforcing knowledges and subjectivities in the technocultural milieu of postmodern societies" (p. 81). In his own teaching, Gough uses narrative theory in innovative ways to open environmental and science education to other stories by rereading them through postmodern science fiction. This could also work with technology education and educational technology, remapping the stories from other positions, and vice versa, so that the historicity and materiality of the textual practices are made visible.

> we coyotes don't deal much with maps   and mapping   so we don't get caught up in scale and orientation and interpreting symbols   we don't deal a lot with territory either   we just go where we go   when we go   as we go   it's not hard   the word 'territory' these days seems to beg the appearance of its consort 'map'   if there's no map then what becomes of territory?   if there's just territory then what reason is there to have a word for it   sometimes those university experts get caught up in binaries   they're running fast but toward what and on what path?   there's a lakota saying   "good thing you're moving slow 'cause you're going the wrong direction

As educators, we can begin with our own schooling, and ourselves, being self-critical and having the courage to deal with controversial issues and the "problems in teaching about this legacy when it is critical of the school subjects themselves" (Willinsky, 1998, p. 257).

For example, the technology education students in this study and myself remapped the story they had been given about *control technologies*. We considered what the story of control technologies might look like if it were told by women of colour working in sweatshops, by women in Africa on the receiving end of western reproductive technologies, by First Nations women who have been sterilized, by Indigenous Peoples whose genes are being stolen, and by those of us who are finding that we have no choice about eating genetically modified foods because there is no mandatory labeling. We talked about the control and eradication of First Peoples in Australia, Canada, and the USA, through the use of guns and biotechnologies, such as smallpox, enforced abortion and birth control, and sterilization. We thought about how these stories might reshape the history of technology offered in schools. We talked about the ongoing forced removals of Indigenous peoples off their traditional lands so that multinational corporations can extract oil and gas, or minerals, or destroy the rainforest to grow coffee beans for Starbucks and raise cattle for McDonald's. The other three categories articulated for technology education, power and energy technologies, production technologies, and manufacturing technologies, are also control technologies and just as implicated in state, corporate, and military control technologies. The students and I discussed how their curriculum is itself a control technology, a particular story articulated from a particular cultural community prescribing what technology is, and is not, as well as what they are to learn about technology. The students began to see their place in the story as little more than docile recipients, rather than as co-narrators of their own learning. They became excited as they examined the unbalanced emphasis on industrial technologies and design and making to the detriment of other equally important conversations on technology, and as they reformulated a more inclusive and complex technological literacy outside the box of prescribed curriculum. They took great joy in creating a place for themselves as they exceeded and transgressed the prescribed meanings of the curriculum so that they were able to migrate and mutate into other meanings and make other connections with other realities, other stories. They began to realize that life, including their own lives, beyond the confines of the prescribed categories, cannot be captured and categorized into universals and standards, statistics, and percentages.

Such storytelling moves away from the abstract dissemination of facts, encouraging students to see and feel their relationship, their implicatedness, in these matters. It connects spirit, body, and land. For Walter Benjamin:

> Storytelling...does not aim to convey the pure essence of the thing, like information or a report. It sinks the thing into the life of the storyteller, in order to bring it out of [her/]him again. Thus traces of the storyteller cling to the story the way the handprints of the potter cling to the clay vessel. (1968, pp. 91–92)

Verena Andermatt Conley (1993) writes that "through the telling of a story, through enunciation itself, the speaker establishes a place and commands a relation to time and space" (p. 88). Story is a form of mediation, a reflection of reality, always adaptive and open to imagination from imposed forms of closure (Minh-ha, 1990). The mediator-storyteller becomes a creator, teacher, and learner. However, with the decrease of technology in the form of the written word as craft, Benjamin is concerned that the art of storytelling as embodied experiences is coming to an end. This erosion is particularly evident in schools with heavy emphasis on the visual, as education becomes more and more tethered to psychoanalysis, virtuality, and business agendas, diminishing the communicability of experience between the eye, the hand, other senses, the spiritual essence of humans, and all life that surrounds us. This development has been particularly devastating for Aboriginal peoples whose orality has been doubly silenced—first by colonization and colonial education, and now reduced to spectacle, to www. This information age is an exchange of embodied, multidimensional experiences for a world of virtual multimedia experiences reduced to a time-space compression—world as surface/screen marked by a profusion of fragmented bits and bytes, force feedings, IVs, free of mastication and/or rumination. As Neil Postman (1993) writes, "information is dangerous when it has no place to go, when there is no theory to which it applies, no pattern in which it fits, where there is no higher purpose that it serves" (p.

63). With a growing reliance on techno-toys, baubles, and prosthetics, we humans are radically changing our senses as well as devaluing and substituting storytelling and experience for information. Those of us who have access to computer technologies speed along with/in the hyperreality of the 'information highway,' virtually without movement, abled and disabled by a proliferation of digitized, byte-sized information bits. We are communicating with each other like never before—or so we believe.

> *raven   I sent you 16 emails yesterday and you didn't answer one   I forwarded 64 listserv messages   and you haven't even gotten back to me about my new webpage   I called you 38 times on my cellphone   even faxed you*
>
> *coyote   I would have responded but I don't have a telephone or fax or computer   my apology for inconveniencing you*
>
> *it's not good enough!   I need to communicate!   it's not a one-way street you know   you have to do your share   buy buy*

Changing the re-visioning angles from arrogant and self-referential reflections to more modest and shared storytelling practices would invite and embrace a diversity of knowledge communities, and stimulate disruption and remapping of technology discourses toward a more equitable, habitable, and sustainable world for all people, other living things, and the environment.

> *now you're dreaming   I've watched human beings in the 'old world' for millennia and their heads always get in the way   it's replaced 'gut feeling'   once pride of individuality took over from pride of connection pride of community   they started getting out the paper and making maps and selling bread   selling food!   imagine that!*

Donna Haraway's (1994) metaphor of "diffraction" provides an important optical tool and narrative strategy. Rather than engage a merely self-referential and mirroring reflective storytelling practice, diffraction evokes a colourful array of stories, those unseeable/unhearable through western frames and the white light of the *one true story* of technology. Diffraction enlivens interrelationships among a diversity of situated knowledges rather than the "god-trick" (Haraway, 1991c) seminal-universalizing knowledge claims for everyone everywhere. With diffraction, the *uni*verse breaks into a kaleidoscopic "*multi*verse" (Gough, 1994a), a polyphony of lively languages attuned to, and alive with, the tensions, resonances, and complicities of diverse local knowledges effecting more heterogeneous accounts of technology and of the world.

> *once diffraction moved from appreciation of a rainbow to looking for gold under it and looking for a means for light amplification through stimulated emission of radiation and star wars   well I could tell that the search for 'pure' knowledge put another massive layer of bullshit between 'the way it is' and the taxpayers who fund these programmes*
>
> *coyote   I don't think you should use words like that in a book for the open market*
>
> *are people so afraid of that word 'pure'?   then how about 'laundered'?*

Equivalency of Epistemologies

> It's not the patriarchal, racial formations of technology education that will engender a revolutionary agency. And it's certainly not the new competitive, economic maximizing, self-interested, yet democratic individual that has been constructed in technology education who will act to confront capitalism, colonialism, consumerism, globalism, homophobia, racism, sexism, and technocentrism in cultural practice. (Petrina, 2000b, p. 200)

Technology curriculum stories are human inventions with complex political, social, and cultural histories. Educators need to do more than compress the study of technology into standards and virtual realities. We need to awaken and enliven technology stories in education, bringing them to a state of intensity so that they can become multiple, dispersed, open, conjunctive, evolving, and alive as a dynamic process of complexity. We need to enact a "multi-storied" (Gough,1993) conversation so that technology education can become an equitable, socially just, intercultural, and environmentally responsible area of study. If the study of technology in schools is to be for all students, then a critical deconstruction of the political, epistemological, methodological, and pedagogical rhetoric used to justify current technology discourses needs to be undertaken with a vastly more diverse cultural community. The conversation(s) need to be composed on the outside of the re/en/trenched solidarity of current technology discourses, in the fuzziness and fluctuation of the diversity and multiplicity of relations in the world. It is not just reforming what exists that is needed, but undertaking a complete overhaul. A rewrite rather than copy edit. It is now time to acknowledge the obvious shortcomings of current technology curricula and make room for the values, practices, and protocols of those left out of curriculum design and in all aspects of education. This will require uncoupling from technocapitalism, as well as decolonizing and Aboriginalizing curricula to strengthen the participation of those currently marginalized.

Mary Bryson (1994) suggests an "ethics of narration":

> Probably the most important job for researchers concerned to understand the scope and limits of the educational uses of technology is to seek out those stories that are not being circulated, to stop "making sense," to look for educational technology's version of Foucault's "subjugated knowledges" within which the complications, contradictions and complexities of this new educational domain are most likely and most productively to be discerned. For it will most likely be in these tales, we suspect, that radically innovative possibilities for the transformation of hegemonic practices might best be found. (p. 6)

coyotes know all about subjugated knowledges and subjugating knowledges when they build a better mousetrap nobody ever asks us   when they do all their 'wild/life' preservation or resource management they don't consult us   they even try to collar us with telemetry and put silicon chips on our ears but we put the bite on that

Revisioning needs to be done from outside the disciplines, and from those inside who are committed to equity, cultural diversity, social justice, and protection of the environment. Pat Thomson (1998) suggests "negotiated curriculum" and "inverted curriculum" as more contingent and permeable alternatives to the current curriculum reforms that are instances of amnesia and myopia. This approach entails curriculum design with and from the knowings of the students and their communities. An important part of the empirical dimension of this study was to acknowledge and encourage the high school and graduate student co-participants to take some of the responsibility for what goes on in their schooling.

From my own experience, students, if given a chance, want to become active participants in this curricular conversation. "Students could collaborate and co-write with a member of the community materials for use in the life of the community, all of which could advance the degree of cultural exchange and understanding between community and school" (Willinsky, 1998, p. 158).

> talking about cultural exchange in canada or the usa   it is like a tsunami inviting a dewdrop to join forces
>
> or an indigenous person negotiating with an 'indian expert'   or introduced eurovirus

Who might the community members be? Gough (1994b) cautions that western intellectuals must not "import ecopolitical wisdom from the narratives of others," rather we might do "comparative readings [listenings, if oral cultures]" (p. 201) of other ways of taking up the world.

> I guess utopia is where you find it rather than construct it   sometimes the biscuit just has to be bitten and you abide by the circumstances
>
> coyote do you mean giving in?
>
> meaning 'yield' if yielding works   otherwise get out of the way

Shohat and Stam (1994) write of "polycentric multiculturalism" as a global politics of culture which has nothing to do with romanticizing or embracing cultures not your own, but learning "at least to recognize it, acknowledge it, take it into account, be ready to be transformed by it" (p. 359). This is no simple thing to undertake. For example, when I spoke with the technology education students about *control technologies* they had to reconsider the history of western imperialism. Some experienced disruptions and dislocations of meaning as we relativized the asymmetry of western privilege and power. This defamiliarization process was experienced by some as "shock, an outrage, giving rise to hysterical discourse of besieged civility and reverse victimization." There were a few who already knew the violence in their bodies and were less upset, although ashamed at their complacency and complicity. Polycentric multiculturalism is not an easy task:

> A radical, polycentric multiculturalism...cannot simply be 'nice,' like a suburban barbeque to which a few token people of color are invited. Any substantive multiculturalism has to recognize the existential realities of pain, anger, and resentment, since the multiple cultures invoked by the term "multiculturalism" have not historically coexisted in relations of equality and mutual respect. It is therefore not merely a question of communicating across borders but discerning the forces, which generate the borders in the first place. Multiculturalism has to recognize not only difference but even better, irreconcilable difference. (pp. 358–359)

Trinh T. Minh-ha (1990) cautions that "the margins, our sites for survival, become our fighting grounds and their site for pilgrimage" (p. 330), and bell hooks (1990) argues that the "margins not to be collapsed, they are important positions, to recover ourselves and move in solidarity to erase the category colonized/colonizer" (p. 342). This is often critiqued as an essentialist stance by those in the dominant culture who are living in very different histories, bodies, and lived realities. This is not an either/or position, but a both/and, a doubled move, shapeshifting for survival and life.

Collaborative efforts are often part of the problem because the ethics and protocols of western communities are not the same as the ethics and protocols of Indigenous communities. It is not simply the plurality of discourse that is needed; we need to concern ourselves with the differential power relations of plurality. For example, to take any story out of an Aboriginal context without the consensus of the community changes it from *story* to acontextual, ahistorical *information*. Robert Bringhurst, for example, has been strongly criticized by the Haida Gwai'i of British Columbia for publishing the stories he took from one member of their community without first seeking permission of the whole community. His stories do not reflect the Haida Gwai'i, their stories, their land, their spirit. Aboriginal stories are not publicly owned assets/utilities; they are not part of the public domain of free enterprise/capitalism. Furthermore, some Aboriginal stories cannot be shared at this time. As Cecil King (1998), Odawa Anishinaabe, from Manitoulin Island, writes:

> It is our responsibility to preserve the flame for humanity, and at the moment it is too weak to be shared, but if we all are still and respect the flame it will grow and thrive in the caring hands of those who hold it. In

time we can all warm ourselves at the fire. But now we have to nurture the flame or we will all lose the gift. (p. 119)

I am concerned about the western assumption of the "right to know" other: my right to know, the students' right to know, the academy's right to know, and especially the right of those who know to not share what they know. My partner is constantly asked to guest lecture about First Nations epistemologies, to do a show and tell. If he does not do stereotypical 'Indian' talk the audience becomes restless. Where are the feathers, where is the smudge bowl? Where does permission reside with respect to the right to know? Has it multiple residences? Is it nomadic, rhizomatic? How is this different from previous ages of discovery and exploration? Who is mapping whom? Who is doing the de- and reterritorializing? Who carries the transit, survey stakes, flags, marking instruments, and fieldbook? Is it the elite: the academy, the courts, the legislature and its agents, or is it the poor, the powerless? What is the direction of learning? of teaching?

Frédérique Apffel-Marglin (1998), with PRATEC (*Proyecto Andino de Technologias Campesinas*, Andean Project of Peasant Technologies), writes that the professionalization of knowledge has made it a commodity, as well as an individual pursuit that "is the very condition of the commodification of knowledge, which is why it is so strictly taught at all levels of education...where rules and regulations polic[e] the individualized production of knowledge" (p. 19). This is so for western curricula. Learning has come to mean the cognitive disengagement from land and spirit. This way of taking up the world is not part of the traditional culture of the Mkamba people of Kenya, or the Lower Stl'atl'imx of British Columbia, or the Mohawk of Tyendinaga, or other Indigenous communities practicing their traditional ways. As Grimaldo Vasquez Rengifo (1998) writes "wisdom for the Andean people is not associated with an accumulation of knowledge—to know a lot about many things—rather, it is associated with the attribute of nurturing, where the sensitivity to know how to nurture is as important as knowing how to allow oneself to be nurtured" (p. 174). Nurturing is not the sole prerogative of humans; it is living respectfully and reciprocally within the world. Eduardo Fernandez Grillo

(1998), also a member of PRATEC, refers to such engagement as living "equivalency":

> Each one of the beings who inhabits this living Andean world is equivalent to every one else; that is, every one (be it man, tree, stone) is a person, complete and indispensable, with its own and inalienable way of being, with its definite personality, its own name, with its specific responsibility in the keeping of the harmony of the world. It is in such condition of equivalence that this living world relates with each one of the others. (p. 224)

you know raven   every wo/man tree stone might be a person   but is every coyote a stone   is every person a tree   which way do the equal signs go for coyotes?   we see people as people   trees as trees   we don't assign one thing to another community   how equal is equal?

don't get caught up in human language coyote   it's never been good for you

Equivalency might be a difficult thing to learn for those schooled in western ways that differentiate humans and other living things, and treat Eurocentric ways as being superior. Living equivalency is nonoppositional and nonvindictive; it refuses a victim stance. It is not about gaining concessions from the state, or validity from the academy, or creating universal truths. Neither does it preclude alliances and dialogical coalitions with those schooled in western ways; it is not a wholly anti-imperialist or anti-colonialist metanarrative. It is, however, a means of breaking a long history of silences. Equivalency is a regeneration of traditional knowings. Regeneration is not to be confused with emancipatory or liberatory pedagogies. "Regeneration is not transformation. The dynamic of regeneration emerges from the attitude of loving the world, as it is, as a parent loves a child, not wanting to transform him or her into someone else" (Apffel-Margin, 1998, p. 40). Practicing equivalency of epistemologies in education would offer different possibilities to those who desperately want to better their lives and feel that the only way out for themselves and their children is to put their cultural knowings aside and learn the ways of the dominant society.

Not only must cultural genocide come to an end, it needs to be seen coming to an end. There needs to be an awakening from standards and hyperrealities to the incredible richness and diversity of the world, and the sensibilities and realities which can no longer be ignored. There needs to be a willingness to make major changes in the so-called freedom and democracy of the West.

> I've seen a steady deterioration in aboriginal freedom and democracy since the settlers landed 500 odd years back   and an equally steady increase of the settlers' rights with respect to making it legal for them to steal aboriginal knowledges and practices by institutes of postknowing and their indian experts   same old song   except this time they're also stuffing words in our mouths that never came from our lungs or vocal cords   op cit

A hot topic in the academy today is TEK (traditional ecological knowledge), which is basically a Euro-American simulacrum, that presumes to encompass or represent the wisdom, spirituality, science, and technologies of Aboriginal Peoples. It is not Aboriginal scholars who are vetting, who are promoting this TEK talk. The tacit assumption seems to be that Aboriginal Peoples' knowledges are there for the taking (read pilfering, larcening, despoiling) and that Aboriginal Peoples are obliged to share these knowledges with the dominant society to save the earth from the extinction or the threat of it, that has been facilitated by western technologies and practices. The dominant society has the power and the knowledge to save the earth—today. It does not need to look elsewhere for solutions. The West needs only to examine itself, analyze itself, discover itself, then *take responsibility* for its own past, present, and future actions, rather than looking at "other" yet again for salvation.

What if western knowledge-making had no borders constructing other, to know in order to study, objectify, act upon, validate or transform? What if the cultural borders were porous, equipped with a reciprocating two-way flow and automatic valve? Learning and teaching would move beyond curriculum writer/teacher desires and designs and a focus on 'the individual.' They would become worlds to cohabit and participate in, collectively made, involving mutually accepted conversations, nurturing life-spaces, opening to not only people, but to all living things, including things orthodox western science tells us are not living. Learning and teaching would become spaces to make decisions about the kind of world we want to live in so that global hypercapitalism and virtual realities are not the only choices. Thes life-spaces would be shared with other epistemologies, methodologies, technologies, and protocols in respectful ways leading toward a fuller presence in the world. This would require a life-long commitment and learning to converse with our whole body, relearning how to dance to the annual cycles of life, restoring an intimacy with the world. "Love's knowledge, to be sure, not reason's, but knowledge still" (Bruns, 1994, p. 210). Nurturing and being nurtured. Perhaps then, there can be a cultural politics of difference that is neither oppositional nor transgressive, a place for more loving, thoughtful, and caring technology discourses. Perhaps technological literacy in education might mean more than industrial and computer technologies, and include *as equivalent conversations* technologies of everyday survival (e.g., nutrition, home repair, sewing); technologies of nurturance (e.g., childcare, care of the elderly, personal and community well-being); technologies of sustainability (organic gardening, permaculture, clean land, water, and air); technologies of the land that are more than the perimeter of western horizons; technologies of spirituality; and technologies of peace.

I unfold my map for this journey, remember and feel the lines and textures of the routes I have taken in my work and play to join landscape and epistemologies in education.

one true story
male western universals
capitalism control consumption
hi tech prediction cognition
value-neutrality production progress
more one true stories
feminisms Marxism antiracisms
ableism gay/lesbian theories body
power differentials power of alliance
'post'colonialisms diversity ambiguity
cyborgology imaginings environment
chaos multiplicity irony complexity
rhizomatics chance operations poethics
an intercultural conversation
decolonization otherwise elsewhere silence spirit
aboriginalization trickster discourse equivalency land
skennen ama sqit mitakuye oyasin we are all related

I look forward to many more journeys, and wonder how many of you I might meet along the way. I load up my canoe, take a long breath of the cool mountain air, and begin paddling to the next plateau.

kukwstum   coyote!

nia:wen   raven!

References

Anderson, L. (1994). *Stories from the nerve bible; A retrospective 1972–1992.* New York: HarperPerennial.

Apffel-Marglin, F. (Ed.). (1998). *The spirit of regeneration: Andean culture confronting Western notions of development.* London & New York: St. Martin's Press.

Bastone, C. (1995). *Transgressing the technocratic culture of technology education: Dominant and other stories of teacher, technology, curricula, and teaching.* Unpublished master's thesis. University of British Columbia, Vancouver, Canada.

Benjamin, C. (1997). Biopiracy and native knowledge: Indigenous rights on the last frontier. *Native Americas, Akwe:kon's Journal of Indigenous Issues, 14*(2), 22–31.

Benjamin, W. (1968). The storyteller: Reflections on the works of Nikolai Leskov. In *Illuminations* (pp. 83–109). New York: Schocken Books.

Bensmaia, R. (1994). On the concept of minor literature from Kafka to Kateb Yacine. In C. V. Boundas & D. Olkowski (Eds.), *Deleuze and the theatre of philosophy* (pp. 213–228). New York: Routledge.

Best, S., & Kellner, D. (2001). *The postmodern adventure: Science, technology, and cultural studies at the end of the millennium.* New York: Guilford Press.

———. (1991). *Postmodern theory: Critical interrogations.* New York: Guilford Press.

Bishop, R. (1998a). Freeing ourselves from neo-colonial domination in research: A Moari approach to creating knowledge. *Qualitative Studies in Education, 11*(2), 199–219.

———. (1998b). *New metaphors for educational practice.* Paper presented at the Annual Conference of the New Zealand Association for Research in Education, Dunedin, New Zealand. December 6–8.

Bobiwash, R. (2001). *The Fourth World: Site of struggle and resistance in the fight against global capital.* Statement to the World Social Forum, Porto Allegre, Brasil.

Borgmann, A. (1984). *Technology and the character of contemporary life.* Chicago: The University of Chicago Press.

Bowers, C. A. (2002). Toward a cultural and ecological understanding of curriculum. In W. E. Doll, Jr. & N. Gough (Eds.), *Curriculum visions* (pp. 75–85). New York: Peter Lang Publishing, Inc.

Braidotti, R. (2002). *Metamorphoses: Towards a materialist theory of becoming.* Cambridge: Polity Press.

———. (1994a). *Nomadic subjects: Embodiment and sexual difference in contemporary feminist theory.* New York: Columbia University Press.

———. (1994b). Toward a new nomadism: Feminist Deleuzian tracks; or, metaphysics and metabolism. In C. V. Boundas & D. Olkowski (Eds.), *Deleuze and the theatre of philosophy* (pp. 187–212). New York: Routledge.

Braundy, M., O'Riley, P., & Petrina, S. (2000). Missing XX chromosomes or gender in/equity in design and technology education? The case of British Columbia. *Journal of Industrial Technology Education, 37*(3), 54–92.

Bright, W. (1993). *A coyote reader.* Berkeley: University of California Press.

British Columbia Ministry of Education. (2002). *Prescribed Learning Outcomes.* Retrieved July 9, 2002, from http://www.bced.gov.bc.ca/irp/curric/lo.html.

———. (1995a). *Environmental concepts in the classroom: A guide for teachers.* Victoria, BC: Author.

———. (1995b). *Technology education 8 to 10: Integrated resource package 1995.* Victoria, BC: Author.

———. (1992). *Technology education: Primary through graduation curriculum/ assessment framework.* Victoria, BC: Author.

Bruns, G. L. (1994). Poethics: John Cage and Stanley Cavell at the crossroads of ethical theory. In M. Perloff & C. Junkerman (Eds.), *John Cage: Composed in America* (pp. 206–225). Chicago, IL: University of Chicago Press.

Bryson, M. (1994). *New technologies/new practices? Teachers as Luddites in/deed.* Paper presented at the annual conference of the American Educational Research Association, New Orleans, April 4–6.

Bryson, M. & de Castell, S. (1998). New technologies, gender, and the cultural ecology of primary schooling: Imagining teachers as Luddites in/deed. *Educational Policy, 12*(5), 542–567.

———. (1996). Learning to make a difference: Gender, new technologies, and in/equity. *Mind, Culture and Activity, 2*(1), 3–21.

Cage, J. (1994). Overpopulation and art. In M. Perloff & C. Junkerman (Eds.), *John Cage: Composed in America* (pp. 14–38). Chicago: University of Chicago Press.

———. (1961). *Silence*. Middletown: Wesleyan University Press.

Carroll, D. (1982). *The subject in question*. Chicago: The University of Chicago Press.

Churchill, W. (1998). *A little matter of genocide: Holocaust and denial in the Americas 1492 to present*. Winnipeg: Arbeiter Ring Publishing.

Clinton, W. (1997). *State of the Union Address*. Washington.

———. (1996). *State of the Union Address*. Washington.

Cole, P. (2002). aboriginalizing methodology: considering the canoe. *Qualitative Studies in Education, 15*(4), 447–459.

———. (2000a). *First Nations knowings as legitimate discourse in education: Coming home to the village*. Unpublished doctoral dissertation, Simon Fraser University, Burnaby, Canada.

———. (2000b). *Navigating around the 'Indian experts' in education: Paddling upstream*. Paper presented at the Annual Symposium on Native Studies, Kingston, November 8–9.

———. (1996). *Body/word as somoto/geo/logo/topo/graphy: Pre/positioning the wor/l/d/self*. Paper presented at the Curriculum as Narrative/Narrative as Curriculum: Lingering in the Spaces Conference, Vancouver, May 2–4.

Cole, P., & O'Riley, P. (2002). Much rezadieu about (Dewey's) goats in the curriculum: Looking back on tomorrow yesterday. In W. E. Doll, Jr. & N. Gough (Eds.), *Curriculum visions* (pp. 132–148). New York: Peter Lang Publishing, Inc.

Conley, V. A. (1993). Eco-subjects. In Verena Andermatt Conley (Ed.), *Rethinking technologies* (pp. 77–91). Minneapolis: University of Minnesota Press.

Cowan, R. S. (1979). From Virginia dare to Virginia Slims: Women and technology in American life. *Technology and Culture, 20*(1), 51–63.

Crnkovic, G. P. (1994). Utopian America and the language of silence. In M. Perloff & C. Junkerman (Eds.), *John Cage: Composed in America* (pp. 167–187). Chicago: University of Chicago Press.

Damarin, S. K. (1994). *Would you rather be a cyborg or a goddess? On being a teacher in a postmodern century.* Paper presented at the Annual Conference of the American Educational Research Association, New Orleans, April 4–8.

———. (1993). Technologies of the individual: Women and subjectivity in the age of information. *Research in Philosophy and Technology, 13, Technology and Feminism,* 183–196.

———. (1993, March). Schooling and situated knowledge: Travel or tourism? *Educational Technology,* 27–32.

Deleuze, G. (1995). *Negotiations* (M. Joughin, Trans.). New York: Columbia University Press. (Original work published 1990)

———. (1994a). *Difference & repetition* (P. Patton, Trans.). New York: Columbia University Press. (Original work published 1968)

———. (1994b). He stuttered. In C. V. Boundas & D. Olkowski (Eds.), *Deleuze and the theatre of philosophy* (pp. 23–29). New York: Routledge.

Deleuze, G., & Guattari, F. (1987). *A thousand plateaus: Capitalism and schizophrenia* (B. Massumi, Trans.). Minneapolis: University of Minnesota Press. (Original work published 1980)

Doll, W. E. Jr. (2002). In E. D. Carlson and T. Oldenski (Eds.), *Educational yearning: The journey of the spirit and democratic education* (pp. 10–21). New York: Peter Lang Publishing, Inc.

Duelli Klein, R. (1987). What's 'new' about the 'new' reproductive technologies? In G. Corea et al (Eds.), *Man-made women: How new reproductive technologies affect women* (pp. 64–73). New York: Harper & Row.

Ellul, J. (1990). *The technological bluff.* Grand Rapids: Wm. B. Eerdmans Publishing Co.

Erdrich, L. (1993). *Love medicine.* New York: HarperPerennial.

Faulkner, W., & E. Arnold. (1985). *Smothered by invention: Technology in women's lives.* London: Pluto Press.

Foster, H. (1985). *Recodings—Art, spectacle, and cultural politics.* Seattle: Bay Press.

Foucault, M. (1983). Preface to *Anti-oedipus: Capitalism and Schizophrenia.* Minneapolis: Minnesota University Press.

———. (1980). *Power/knowledge: Selected interviews and other writings, 1972–1977* (C. Gordon, Ed.). New York: Pantheon Books.

———. (1979). *Discipline & punish* (A. Sheridan, Trans.). New York: Vintage Books. (Original work published 1975)

Franklin, U. (1999). *The real world of technology*. Toronto, ON: House of Anansi.

Fuentes, A., & Ehrenreich, B. (1988). *Women in the global factory*. Boston: South End Press.

Gabilondo, J. (1995). Postcolonial cyborgs: Subjectivity in the age of cybernetic reproduction. In C. Hables Gray (Ed.), *The cyborg handbook* (pp. 423–432). New York: Routledge.

Game, A. (1991). *Undoing the social: Towards a deconstructive sociology*. Toronto: University of Toronto Press.

Garson, B. (1988). *The electronic sweatshop: How computers are transforming the office of the future into the factory of the past*. New York: Penguin Books.

Gordon, C. (Ed.). (1980). *Power/knowledge: Selected interviews and other writings, 1972–1977 by Michael Foucault*. London: Harvester Wheatsheaf.

Goshorn, K. A. (1994). Valorizing 'the feminine' while rejecting feminism — Baudrillard's feminist provocations. In D. Kellner (Ed.), *Baudrillard: A critical reader* (pp. 257–291). Oxford: Blackwell.

Gough, A. (1997). *Education and the environment: Policy, trends and the problems of marginalisation*. Melbourne: The Australian Council for Educational Research.

Gough, N. (1998). All around the world: Science education, constructivism, and globalization. *Educational Policy, 12*(5), 507–524.

———. (1997). Weather™ Incorporated: Environmental education, postmodern identities, and technocultural constructions of nature. *Canadian Journal of Environmental Education, 2*, 145–162.

———. (1995). Manifesting cyborgs in curriculum inquiry. *Melbourne Studies in Education, 29*(1): 71–83.

———. (1994a). Narration, reflection, diffraction: Aspects of fiction in educational inquiry. *Australian Educational Researcher, 21*(3), 47–76.

———. (1994b). Playing at catastrophe: Ecopolitical education after poststructuralism. *Educational Theory, 44*(2), 189–210.

———. (1993). Environmental education, narrative complexity and postmodern science/fiction. *International Journal of Science Education, 15*(5), 607–625.

Grady, W. (1994). *The nature of coyotes*. Vancouver: Greystone Books.

Gregory, D. (1993). *Geographical imaginations*. Cambridge: Blackwell Publishers.

Grillo, E. F. (1998). Development or cultural affirmation in the Andes? In F. Apffel-Marglin (Ed.), *The spirit of regeneration: Andean culture confronting Western notions of development* (pp. 124-145). London: St. Martin's Press.

Grossman, K. (1993). Environmental racism. In S. Harding (Ed.), *The racial economy of science: Toward a democratic future* (pp. 326-334). Bloomington: Indiana University Press.

Grosz, E. A. (1995). *Space, time, and perversion: Essays on the politics of bodies*. New York: Routledge.

―――. (1994). A thousand tiny sexes: Feminism and rhizomatics. In C. V. Boundas & D. Olkowski (Eds.), *Deleuze and the theatre of philosophy* (pp. 187-212). New York: Routledge.

―――. (1992). Bodies—Cities. In B. Colomina (Ed.), *Sexuality & space* (pp. 241-254). Princeton: Princeton Architectural Press.

Guattari, F. (1995). *Chaosophy*. New York: Semiotext(e).

Hacker, S. (1989). *Pleasure, power & technology*. London: Unwin Hyman, Inc.

Haraway, D. J. (1997). *Modest _ Witness @ Second _ Millennium.FemaleMan© _ Meets_OncoMouse™*. New York: Routledge.

―――. (1995). Cyborgs and symbionts: Living together in the New World Order. In C. Hables Gray (Ed.), *The cyborg handbook* (pp. xi-xx). New York: Routledge.

―――. (1994). A game of cat's cradle: Science studies, feminist theory, cultural studies. *Configurations: A Journal of Literature, Science, and Technology, 2*(1), 59-71.

―――. (1992). The promises of monsters: A regenerative politics for inappropriate/d others. In L. Grossberg, C. Nelson & P. Treichler (Eds.), *Cultural studies* (pp. 295-337). New York: Routledge.

―――. (1991a). The actors are cyborg, nature is coyote, and the geography is elsewhere: Postscript to "Cyborgs at large." In C. Penley & A. Ross (Eds.), *Technoculture* (pp. 21-26). Minneapolis: University of Minnesota Press.

―――. (1991b). Cyborgs at large: An interview with Donna Haraway. In C. Penley & A. Ross (Eds.), *Technoculture* (pp. 1-20). Minneapolis: University of Minnesota Press.

———. (1991c). *Simians, cyborgs, and women: The reinvention of nature* (pp. 183–201). New York: Routledge.

———. (1989). *Primate visions: Gender, race, and nature in the world of modern science.* New York: Routledge.

———. (1985). Manifesto for cyborgs: Science, technology, and socialist feminism in the 1980s. *Socialist Review, 80,* 65–108.

Harding. S. (1986). *The science question in feminism.* Ithaca: Cornell University Press.

Harvey, D. (1989). *The condition of postmodernity.* Cambridge: Basil Blackwell.

Hayles, N. K. (1995). The life cycle of cyborgs: Writing the posthuman. In C. H. Gray (Ed.), *The cyborg handbook* (pp. 321–335). New York: Routledge.

———. (1994). Chance operations: Cagean paradox and contemporary science. In M. Perloff & C. Junkerman (Eds.), *John Cage: Composed in America* (pp. 226–241). Chicago: University of Chicago Press.

———. (1993). The seductions of cyberspace. In V. A. Conley (Ed.), *Rethinking technologies* (pp. 173–190). Minneapolis: University of Minnesota Press.

hooks, b. (1990). Talking back. In R. Ferguson et al (Eds.), *Out there: Marginalization and contemporary cultures* (pp. 337–340). New York: The New Museum of Contemporary Art.

Hudson, D., & DePaoli, M. (1999). *Archaeological investigation of the Six-Mile Site (DkRn 5), Lower Lillooet River, Southwestern British Columbia.* Deroche, BC: In-SHUCK-ch Services Society.

International Technology Education Association. (2000). *Standards for technological literacy: Content for the study of technology.* Reston: Author.

———. (1996). *Technology for all Americans.* Reston: Author.

———. (1990). *A conceptual framework for technology education.* Reston: Author.

Irigary, L. (1993). *Je, tu, nous: Toward a culture of difference* (A. Martin, Trans.). New York & London: Routledge. (Original work published 1990)

Joy, B. (2000, April). Why the future doesn't need us. *Wired.* 238–262.

Kiluva-Ndunda, M. M. (2001). *Women's agency and educational policy: The experiences of the women of Kilome, Kenya.* Albany: State University of New York Press.

King C. (1998). Here come the anthros. In T. Biolsi and L. J. Zimmerman (Eds.), *Indians and anthropologists: Vine Deloria, Jr., and the critique of anthropology* (pp. 115–119). Tucson: The University of Arizona Press.

King, T. (1994). *Green grass, running water.* Toronto: HarperPerennial.

———. (1993). *A Coyote Columbus story.* Toronto: HarperPerennial.

Kramarae, C. (1988). Gotta go Myrtle, technology's at the door. In C. Kramarae (Ed.), *Technology and women's voices: Keeping in touch* (pp. 1–14). New York: Routledge & Kegan Paul.

Kroker, A. (1992). *The possessed individual: Technology and the French postmodern.* Montréal: New World Perspectives.

Kroker, A., & M. A. Weinstein. (1994). *Data trash: The theory of the virtual class.* Montréal: New World Perspectives.

Lather, P. (1996). Troubling clarity: The politics of accessible language. *Harvard Educational Review, 66*(3), 525–544.

———. (1993). Fertile obsession: Validity after poststructuralism. *The Sociological Quarterly, 34*(4), 673–693.

———. (1992). Critical frames in education research: Feminist and post-structural perspectives. *Theory into Practice, xxxi*(2), 87–99.

———. (1991). *Feminist research in education: Within/against.* Geelong, Australia: Deakin University Press.

Leto, V. (1988). 'Washing seems it's all we do': Washing technology and women's communication. In C. Kramarae (Ed.), *Technology and women's voices: Keeping in touch* (pp. 161–179). New York: Routledge & Kegan Paul.

Lingis, A. (1994). The society of dismembered body parts. In C. V. Boundas & D. Olkowski (Eds.), *Deleuze and the theatre of philosophy* (pp. 289–303). New York: Routledge.

Martin, L. H., Gutman, H. & Hutton, P. H. (1988). *Technologies of self: A Seminar with Michel Foucault.* Amherst: The University of Massachusetts Press.

Massumi, B. (1992). *A users' guide to capitalism and schizophrenia: Deviations from Deleuze and Guattari.* Cambridge: The MIT Press.

———. (1987). Translator's foreward: Pleasures of philosophy. In G. Deleuze & F. Guattari, *A thousand plateaus: Capitalism and schizophrenia* (B. Massumi, Trans.) (pp. ix–xv). Minneapolis: University of Minnesota Press. (Original work published 1980)

Minh-ha, T. T. (1990). Cotton and iron. In R. Ferguson et al (Eds.), *Out there: Marginalization and contemporary cultures* (pp. 327–336). New York: The New Museum of Contemporary Art.

———. (1989). *Woman, native, other: Writing postcoloniality and feminism.* Bloomington: Indiana University Press.

Morrison, T. (1992). *Playing in the dark: Whiteness and the literary imagination.* New York, NY: Vintage Books.

Needham, J. (1993). Poverties and triumphs of the Chinese scientific tradition. In S. Harding (Ed.), *The racial economy of science: Toward a democratic future* (pp. 161–179). Bloomington: Indiana University Press.

New Zealand Ministry of Education. (1995). *Technology in the New Zealand Curriculum.* Wellington, NZ: Author.

ndunda, m (1995). *Educational policy: The experiences of the women of Kilome, Kenya.* Unpublished doctoral dissertation. The University of British Columbia, Vancouver, Canada.

Nietzsche, F. (1961). *Thus spoke Zarathustra.* (R. J. Hollingdale, Trans.). New York: Penguin Books.

Noble, D. (1993). The regime of technology in education. *Holistic Education Review, 6*(2), 4–13.

———. (1991). *The classroom arsenal: Military research, information technology, and public education.* New York: Falmer.

Olkowski, D. (1994). Nietzsche's dice throw: Tragedy, nihilism, and the body without organs. In C. V. Boundas & D. Olkowski (Eds.), *Deleuze and the theater of philosophy.* New York: Routledge.

Ontario Ministry of Education. (2000). *Technological Studies: Ontario Curriculum, Grades 11 and 12.* Toronto, ON: Author.

O'Neill, A., & Jolley, S. (1996/1997). Privatising curriculum: Constructing consumer society. The technology curriculum: The politics of food—women's work? To high tech or oblivion. *Delta: Policy and Practice in Education, 1/2*(48/49), 221–248.

O'Riley, P. (1996). A different storytelling of technology education curriculum revisions: A storytelling of difference. *Journal of Technology Education, 7*(2), 28–39.

———. (1994). *Women, space, and knowledge in the 'Information Age': From multidimensional spaces to world as surface/screen.* Paper presented at the annual conference of the American Educational Research Association, New Orleans, April 4–8.

———. (1992). *Contextualizing the gendered and industrial bias of technology education.* Master's thesis, University of British Columbia, Vancouver, Canada.

O'Riley, P., & Scott, D. (1996). Psycho logics: Techno bits and desire bytes in the worlds of virtuality and analysis. *Australian Educational Researcher, 23*(3), 97–107.

Penley, C., & Ross, A. (1991). Cyborgs at large: Interview with Donna Haraway. In C. Penley & A. Ross (Eds.), *Technoculture* (pp. 1–20). Minneapolis: University of Minnesota Press.

Petricic, S. (2002). Computers in the classroom: Does higher tech mean better education? http://www.cbc.ca/national/sasa/computerclass.html.

Petrina, S. (2000a). The political ecology of design and technology education: An inquiry into methods. *International Journal of Technology and Design Education, 10,* 207–237.

———. (2000b). The politics of technological literacy. *International Journal of Technology and Design Education, 10,* 181–206.

———. (1993). Diversity, not uniformity; united, not standardized: A reaction to Wright's 'Challenge to all technology educators'. *Journal of Technology Education, 4*(2), 71–78.

Postman, N. (1996). *The end of education: Re-defining the value of school.* New York: Alfred Knopf.

———. (1993). *Technopoly: The surrender of culture to technology.* New York: Vantage Books.

Quinn, D. (1993). *Ishmael.* New York: Bantam Books.

Rabinow, P. (Ed.). (1984). *The Foucault reader.* New York: Pantheon Books.

Rengifo, G. V. (1998). The *Allyu.* (In F. Apffel-Marglin (Ed.), *The spirit of regeneration: Andean culture confronting Western notions of development* (pp. 89–123). London: St. Martin's Press.

Retallack, J. (1994). Poethics of a complex realism. In M. Perloff & C. Junkerman (Eds.), *John Cage: Composed in America* (pp. 242–273). Chicago: University of Chicago Press.

Robins, K., & Webster, F. (1999). *Times of the technoculture: From the information society to the virtual life*. London: Routledge.

———. (1989). *The technical fix: Education, computers, and industry*. New York: St. Martin's Press.

Ronell, A. (1993) Our narcotic modernity. In V. A. Conley (Ed.), *Rethinking technologies* (pp. 59–73). Minneapolis: University of Minnesota Press.

St. Pierre, E. A. (1997). Methodology in the fold and the irruption of transgressive data. *Qualitative Studies in Education, 10*(2), 175–189.

Sanders, M. E. (1995). Technology for all Americans. *Journal of Technology Education, 6*(2), 2–3.

Sandoval, C. (1995). New sciences: Cyborg feminism and the methodology of the oppressed. In C. H. Gray (Ed.), *The cyborg handbook* (pp. 407–421). New York: Routledge.

Saskatchewan Education. (1988). *Understanding the common essential learnings: A handbook for teachers*. Saskatoon: Author.

Scheurich, J. J. (1996). The masks of validity: A deconstructive investigation. *Qualitative Studies in Education, 9*(1), 49–60.

———. (1995). A postmodernist critique of research interviewing. *Qualitative Studies in Education, 8*(3), 239–252.

Schoonmaker, S. (1994). Capitalism and the Code: A critique of Baudrillard's Third Order Simulacrum. In D. Kellner (Ed.), *Baudrillard: A critical reader* (pp. 168–188). Oxford: Blackwell.

Shohat, E., & Stam, R. (1994). *Unthinking Eurocentrism: Multiculturalism and the media*. London: Routledge.

Serres, M., & Latour, B. (1998). *Conversations on science, culture, and time*. Ann Arbor: Michigan University Press.

Smith, L. T. (1999). *Decolonizing methodologies: Research and Indigenous peoples*. Dunedin, NZ: University of Otago Press.

Snook, I. (1996). *Technology: A new subject or an ideological strategy?* Paper presented at the Annual Conference of the New Zealand Association for Research in Education, Nelson, NZ, December 3–5.

Spivak, G. C. (1990). Explanation and culture: Marginalia. In R. Ferguson et al (Eds.), *Out there: Marginalization and contemporary cultures* (pp. 377–393). New York: The New Museum of Contemporary Art.

———. (1976). Translator's preface. In Jacques Derrida, *Of grammatology*. Baltimore: Johns Hopkins University Press.

Taylor, W. D., & Johnsen, J. B. (1993). *The reduction of teachers and students to components: An essay of technology and classrooms*. Unpublished manuscript, Ohio State University.

Third World Network. (1993). Modern science in crisis: A Third World Response. In S. Harding (Ed.) *The racial economy of science: Toward a democratic future* (pp. 484–518). Bloomington: Indiana University Press.

Thomson, P. (2002). Perspective on Molnar. In W. E. Doll, Jr. & N. Gough (Eds.), *Curriculum visions* (pp. 213–217). New York: Peter Lang Publishing, Inc.

———. (1998). *Doing justice: An Australian cautionary tale about bell curves, outcomes data and language games*. Paper presented at the New Zealand Association for Educational Research Annual Conference, University of Otago, Dunedin, NZ, December 6–8.

United Nations. (2002). *Fighting AIDS: A New Global Resolve*. Retrieved August 15, 2002 from http://www.unaids.org/barcelona/presskit/Barcelona/chapter1.html.

Van Maanen, J. (1988). *Tales of the field: On writing ethnography*. Chicago: University of Chicago Press.

Villenas, S. (2000). This ethnography called my back: Writings of the exotic gaze, "othering" Latina, and recuperating Xicanisma. In E. St. Pierre & W. Pillow (Eds.), *Working the ruins: Feminist poststructural theory and methods in education* (pp. 74–94). New York: Routledge.

Virilio, P. (1999). *Politics of the very worst*. New York: Semiotext(e).

———. (1993). *The third interval: A critical transition*. In V. A. Conley (Ed.), Rethinking technologies (pp. 3–12). Minneapolis: University of Minnesota Press.

Visser, M. (2002). *Beyond fate*. Toronto: House of Anansi Press.

Vizenor, G. (1994). *Manifest manners: Postindian warriors of survivance*. Hanover: Wesleyan University Press.

———. (Ed.). (1993). *Narrative chance: Postmodern discourse on Native American Indian literatures*. Norman: University of Oklahoma Press.

———. (1992). *Dead voices: Natural agonies in the new world*. Norman: University of Oklahoma Press.

———. (1991). *The heirs of Columbus.* Hanover: Wesleyan University Press.

Wajcman, J. (1991). *Feminism confronts technology.* North Sydney: Allen and Unwin.

Watkins, E. (1993). *Throwaways: Work culture & consumer education.* Stanford: Stanford University Press.

Wells, J. (1995). Defining biotechnology. *The Technology Teacher, 54*(7), 11–14.

Wilde, O. (1992). *The Picture of Dorian Gray.* New York: Random House, Inc.

Willinsky, J. (1998). *Learning to divide the world: Education at Empire's end.* Minneapolis: University of Minnesota Press.

Winner, L. (1996). *The handwriting on the wall: Resisting technoglobalism's assault on education.* Unpublished manuscript, Rensselaer Polytechnic Institute, Troy.

Wright, J. V. (1999). *A history of the Native people of Canada, Volume II (1000 B.C.–A.D. 500).* Hull: Canadian Museum of Civilization.

Index

andragogy, 140

becoming, 27–29, 32, 33, 108
becoming nomad, 29

Canis rhizomaticus, 33
chance operations, 36–37
control societies, 26
curriculum, 3–7, 14, 15, 56–65, 73, 76, 146–148, 150, 157
cyborgs, 22, 101–103
    as First World, 111–115
    as narrative experiments, 105–106, 108–109
    and tricksters, 102, 117–119
    cyborg teachers, 104–105

differenciation, 26–27
desire, 1, 8, 25, 27, 32, 110–111
    and education, 33
    desiring-machines, 27
device paradigm, 59
disciplinary societies, 26
discourse of difference, 12
dromospheric pollution, 109

educational technology, 5
    costs, 5
    and business, 100, 136–138
    and environment, 136–137
    and gender, 14, 81, 104–105, 134
    and militarism, 69, 70
    and neocolonialism, 68, 69
    and culture, 106–108, 130
    and socioeconomics, 106–109
    and students' health, 5, 135
    a virtual realities, 5, 67, 72, 100, 134, 136, 139, 156

equivalency of knowledges, 73, 154, 155, 157

fake becoming, 33

hybridity, 101, 116

intercultural conversation, 116, 157

methodology
    Aboriginal, 45, 47
    as self-empowerment, 47
    co-reseaching, 50–52, 153
    dataplay, 22, 121, 139–142
    ethics, 50, 51
    framing, 21, 42–48
    from the land,
    methodology of difference, 22, 51
    Maori, 46
    right to know, 154
    validity, 48–50
    writing plateaux, 17–20
miniaturization, 109
minorizing, 30
    and trickster discourse, 33
    language, 30–32
    technology discourses, 31

narrative chance, 21, 33–36, 39, 96–97
nomadics, 21, 28–30, 39
nurturance, 154, 156, 157

poethics, 21, 37–39
polycentric multiculturalism, 152
posthumans, 22, 101

reciprocity, 154, 156

regeneration, 155
remapping technology discourses, 21, 25, 33, 146, 147, 149
- collaboration, 151–152
- diffraction, 149
- ethics of narration, 151
- multistoried, 150

rhizome, 27-28, 95
rhizomatics, 18, 21, 2433
- and feminism, 28–32
- and trickster discourse, 20, 33–36

rhizopoiesis, 53

silence, 31, 35–37, 39, 50, 133
standardization/universalization, 26, 56, 60, 62–63, 65, 67–69, 140, 150
storytelling, 24, 91, 108, 144, 147–149
- and technology, 108–109
- and technology education, 95–97
- as trickster discourse, 33

students,
- as human capital, 70, 78, 83
- right to know, 97–98
- resistance, 94
- shortchanged, 98

techné as poiesis, 145
technology/technologies,
- Aboriginal, First Nations, Indigenous, 8, 87, 88, 91–93, 156
- and corporate globalization, 6
- and culture, 82–83, 87
- and de-skilling, 109
- and environment, 87–88, 129
- and gender, 81–83, 108–110
- and human rights, 87
- and surveillance, 82
- as the future, 77, 132
- biotechnologies, 75, 82–83
- control technologies, 57–64, 147
- disciplinary, 60

- everyday, 78, 79
- household, 78
- hyperrealities, 34–35
- language as, 6, 13, 24
- of everyday survival, 157
- of the land, 157
- of normalization, 102
- of nurturance, 17, 157
- of peace, 157
- of self, 26, 102
- of spirituality, 157
- of survival, 17
- of sustainability, 17, 59, 73, 157
- reproductive, 75, 82–83
- time/space compression, 107–109, 148

technology discourses,
- Aboriginalizing, 150
- and difference, 26
- and environment, 6,10, 76, 83–86
- and socioeconomics, 6, 50, 59, 63, 150
- and special needs, 46–47
- and global capitalism, 6, 26, 68, 76, 83, 146
- as legacy of imperialism, 8–10, 24, 145
- as manifest manners, 7
- as order-words, 6, 24
- decolonizing, 151
- environmental responsibility, 150

technology education, 4–5
- and capitalism, 60, 64, 65–72
- and culture, 14, 62, 64, 86–95, 98
- and environment, 82–86, 87, 88, 91
- and First Nations, 93–94
- and gender, 1–3, 62, 64, 76, 76–81, 98
- and hegemonic masculinity, 78–79

and military complex, 56, 62, 68–71
and neocolonialism, 8–10, 67–69, 89–95
and socioeconomics, 14, 62, 86–89
as training, 56, 59, 65, 146
computerization of, 64–65, 66
control technologies, 57–59, 147
problem solving, 60–61, 66
educating for consumerism, 5, 65–72
high/low tech, 3, 75, 98
history, 76–78, 144
Maori, 15
prescribed technologies, 6, 11, 56–59, 62–63, 98, 146, 147, 148
revocalization, 58
teaching of us/them, 77, 86–89, 94
technification of, 56–59, 60
trades/technical orientation, 3, 55, 56, 63
technological literacy, 7, 11, 26, 60–61, 147, 157
as computer literacy, 5, 67
traditional ecological knowledge (TEK), 89, 156
trickster discourse, 21, 33–36, 95, 97–98

Studies in the Postmodern Theory of Education

General Editors
Joe L. Kincheloe & Shirley R. Steinberg

Counterpoints publishes the most compelling and imaginative books being written in education today. Grounded on the theoretical advances in criticalism, feminism, and postmodernism in the last two decades of the twentieth century, Counterpoints engages the meaning of these innovations in various forms of educational expression. Committed to the proposition that theoretical literature should be accessible to a variety of audiences, the series insists that its authors avoid esoteric and jargonistic languages that transform educational scholarship into an elite discourse for the initiated. Scholarly work matters only to the degree it affects consciousness and practice at multiple sites. Counterpoints' editorial policy is based on these principles and the ability of scholars to break new ground, to open new conversations, to go where educators have never gone before.

For additional information about this series or for the submission of manuscripts, please contact:
        Joe L. Kincheloe & Shirley R. Steinberg
        c/o Peter Lang Publishing, Inc.
        275 Seventh Avenue, 28th floor
        New York, New York 10001

To order other books in this series, please contact our Customer Service Department:
        (800) 770-LANG (within the U.S.)
        (212) 647-7706 (outside the U.S.)
        (212) 647-7707 FAX

Or browse online by series:
        www.peterlangusa.com